ALSO FROM JASON BROWN

MARGIN MATTERS: HOW TO LIVE ON A SIMPLE BUDGET &
CRUSH DEBT FOREVER

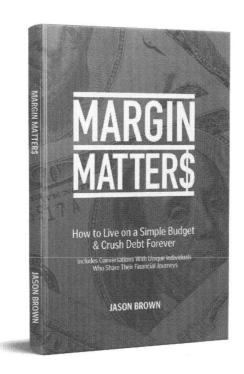

IT IS POSSIBLE!

HOW I EARNED TWO DEBT-FREE DEGREES...
AND HOW YOU CAN, TOO.

JASON BROWN

Edited by
AMETHYST BROWN

Cover designed by Angela Walker

Interior designed by Jason Brown

Edited by Amethyst Brown

Author headshot by Danielle Torrence

Creative Consultants: Angela Hunt and Charlotte Doolin

First Edition

ISBN: 978-1-7332389-2-2

Printed in the United States of America

The Library of Congress Cataloging-in-Publication Data is available upon request.

Website: yourmarginmatters.com

Email: Jason@yourmarginmatters.com

DEDICATION

To my wife and strongest supporter, Amethyst, who paid off $60,000 of student loan debt in two years and transformed the financial future of our family.

To my sons, Maddux and Kameron. I hope you will implement these strategies in your life one day and realize that you are not destined to be saddled with massive amounts of debt.

To my parents, Melvin and Belinda, who demonstrated fiscal responsibility through their choices and actions in life.

And to everyone who dreams of obtaining higher education without being crushed by debt.

Education should not be a DEBT sentence.

CONTENTS

IT IS POSSIBLE!

FOREWORD

By Kyle Behnke

Over the course of 14 years I earned three university degrees and took out student loans for each of them. Before I knew it, I was staring at $170,000 of debt. Had I taken the knowledge I have now and put it back into my 22-year-old self, I would've done things a lot differently.

Upon entering college at Tennessee Tech, I was passionate about working in the racing industry, specifically being a part of a NASCAR team. As a result, I earned a bachelor's degree in mechanical engineering before moving to Orlando and obtaining a master's in industrial engineering from the University of Central Florida's motorsports industrial engineering program.

As I got older my interest in working in the racing industry waned. I came to the realization that even though I held a master's degree in industrial engineering, if I wanted to join a NASCAR team, I would have to spend two-to-three years sweeping floors and working my way up. Additionally, I didn't find being on the road for 30 weekends a year appealing. At that point I had been a broke college kid for about five years and was offered a really good job with a military contractor so I took it.

Although I enjoyed the military contractor position, after nearly eight years I wanted to do my own thing. My true passion is what I'm doing now and that's running a business. I've always wanted to have my own company. To achieve this goal I decided to attend Emory University and get my MBA, which is probably the best degree that I've earned. I'll admit, Emory wasn't cheap and at that point I already had student debt piling up from previous degrees.

My logic was I'm going to take out more student loans to get my MBA but when I come out of that I'll be making $100,000 to $150,000 a year so I'll have no problem paying back the loans in 10 years. Now, here we are almost 10 years later and I'm still paying it off. We have the means now, because of the business, to pay it off, but you don't realize how much the debt grows due to the interest. You can't make a big dent into any debt until you start paying more [than the minimum payment]. My loan payments are similar to what a mortgage payment might be.

The debt from obtaining so many degrees began to add up quickly and I didn't have a great plan to pay for it. Thankfully I was able to refinance my loans to a lower interest rate of 4% after some of them were as high as 8.5% on a federal student loan. The government is making massive profits off those loans, which is why they don't want to forgive them.

It's so hard to make a dent in paying off these student loans. For example, if you have a $1,000 payment you might only be paying off around $150 a month on the principle. It would take you a long time to pay that off. I still have around $150,000 to pay off. Even if I was making a $100,000 a year salary it would be tough to pay for the student loan debt, plus a house, and car payment. At one point, I was paying $2,200 a month. How do you pay that? That's basically like having a $500,000 or $600,000 house!

Someone might want to take on those loans because they want a good education that will help them. Unless you know you're going into a high-paying field or will become some type of entrepreneur down the road where you will have a big payday, or have a six-figure job lined up, then it doesn't make sense to take out that kind of debt. My schooling has helped me, but when you look at the debt—if I was a teacher or civil servant where the jobs don't pay as well—that kind of education cost can hamper you for the rest of your life.

The entire student loan process can be deceiving because it's so easy to sign up for the loans and all of sudden you have $15,000 in your checking account. When you're 21 or 22, you don't really know about interest rates. I didn't have the knowledge and education of financing back then to understand that, "Hey, this is going to end up being a lot of money in 10 years when I have to repay it."

It took me a while to figure out what I was interested in. When I went to school and got into my degree programs, I realized that wasn't what I wanted to do. But at the time everyone is telling you, "You need to go to school, you need to do this, you need to do that." It's hard when you're young and you truly don't know what you want to do or have the experience to do it yet. When I got into the engineering field, I didn't like the tedious work of it. I'm not a detail-oriented guy. I'm better at seeing the broader picture as opposed to the everyday mundane details. I discovered more of a calling to the management side but it took time for me to figure out what I truly enjoyed.

Looking back instead of getting engineering degrees I would've gone into business. I would've gotten a business degree and I think I could've learned a lot from that and it would've gotten me pretty far. Even though I'm not designing things as an engineer, I used a lot of knowledge from my degrees. I took a lot of entrepreneurship, management, and decision analysis classes and they've paid off. All that broad knowledge coupled with the real-world experience makes a big difference. Now, it's debatable if it was worth the $100,000+ that I paid for it and still paying on it. In hindsight, at the time it's difficult to figure out. Some people know what they want to do at 22 and others might not.

If I just had a basic, four-year degree and some vocational experience, I could probably do what I'm doing now. On the other hand, I learned some relevant things in business school with the MBA. I think you just have to ask yourself, "Do I really need that to be successful?" You will meet a lot of entrepreneurs who never finished college. Not everyone's a Mark Zuckerberg but there is some kind of medium of what you want to do.

My advice is to get some experience in the real world. If you are unsure of what you want to do, go work someplace and obtain valuable experience. In doing so you can make good money before you get that college degree and potentially take on student debt. From a business owner's standpoint, the other thing that college doesn't help you with is learning how to deal with people. To go from a classroom to running a business you need some street cred and the ability to deal with all kinds of people. Don't be afraid to take those blue-collar jobs while going through college.

Additionally, make sure you need that degree before you enroll. It's easy to get a $30,000 loan to pay for your school and still have $10,000 left after all your expenses. When you're 20 that seems like a lot of money but in the grand scheme of things it's not. There are a lot of ways to get an education without putting yourself into debt. For me, I've been very fortunate to have a successful business, yet I'm still paying on my student loan debt. Put that into perspective. However, I might be an extreme case because I have three degrees.

If you don't know what you want to do, take your time to think about what you truly want. It wasn't until I got older that I figured out the financial side of things. Had I known then what I know now, I would've taken a different path.

INTRODUCTION

Without a doubt, young people today start their adult lives burdened with much more student loan debt than previous generations. News of the student loan debt crisis continues to permeate our society with the media hyperfocused on the total amount nationally, which continues to rapidly increase. In fact, there are now 45 million borrowers who collectively owe nearly $1.7 trillion in student loan debt in the U.S. As a result, student loan debt is now the second-highest consumer debt category— behind only mortgage debt—and higher than both credit cards and auto loans. The average student loan debt for members of the Class of 2018 is $29,200, a 2% increase from the prior year, according to the Institute for College Access and Success.

Those who say there's a student loan crisis cite, among other issues, the surge in total student loan debt, the complexity of repayment options, the high rejection rate for student loan forgiveness, the difficulty of student loan discharge in bankruptcy, and the challenges with student loan servicers. As reported by CNBC, the average respondent says that it takes 18.5 years to pay off student loans, from age 26 to age 45. The Department of Education reports that the typical repayment period for borrowers with between $20,000 and $40,000 in federal student loans is 20 years.

Is it really a "crisis?"

I asked my economist friend Dr. Steve Petty who said:

> The student loan debt crisis is a bona fide crisis. The 45 million people impacted by their *early-in-life* decision to take on debt to finance higher education represents a very important group of people. To explain, it must be understood that higher education represents human capital investment. This investment pays off best for those who are younger, successful academically, and promptly hired upon graduation without becoming underemployed (accepting a job beneath their skills, training, education, etc.). The payoff is both for the individual and for society (private benefits and spillover benefits) and is the most important aspect of human capital investment. It represents both a higher future income stream for the individual and an additional highly educated citizen that is more likely to participate wisely in marketplaces, pay taxes, and obey the laws of the land—and initiate teachable moments with those around him/her.
>
> Around one-quarter (25%) of the $1.7 trillion is in deferment, forbearance, or default. With COVID-19 taken into account, I wouldn't be surprised if up to half of the $1.7 trillion is in danger of default. This translates to around half of the civilian labor force being straddled if not strangled by student loan debt in 2021. It is a crisis now on top of multiple crises. Unlike COVID-19, there is no vaccine or remedy on the immediate horizon.

Consider the Shocking Statistics

- $1.7 trillion in total U.S. student loan debt
- 45 million Americans with student loan debt
- Nearly 70% of students take out loans to help pay for school
- 11.1% of student loans were 90 days or more delinquent or are in default (pre-pandemic pause)
- The average monthly student loan payment was $300 (pre-pandemic pause)
- Students borrowed an estimated $102 billion for the 2019-20 academic year alone

Sources: Data via the U.S. Federal Reserve, TICAS.org, and the College Board.

The Core Issue

Student loans are not the reason there's a student debt crisis in this country. The loans are simply the symptom of a much bigger issue. The real problem is that there's not adequate education, information, or support systems in place to assist students (and their families) to make smarter college choices while they are still in high school. The issue is threefold: 1) lack of awareness, 2) lack of resources, and 3) most importantly, lack of financial literacy/education.

* * *

Dr. Petty shared with me some of his thoughts on the root problem:

Colleges and universities have not been good stewards of the monies flowing to them for educating our population and carrying out educational and extracurricular activities that promote the general welfare. Instead, colleges and universities contribute way too much to overall inequality in our society.

When I think of the sports/media contracts that deliver millions of dollars to our higher education institutions, it makes me wonder why the lion's share doesn't go back to overall student-centric activities. Hey, why not use sports money to help fund tuition?

This book is a result of being galvanized from constantly hearing about the student loan debt "crisis" and now the building movement for student loan debt "forgiveness." Instead of fighting for Band-Aid solutions, let's educate aspiring college students and their parents on how to avoid student loan debt in the first place. Consider people like my wife Amethyst who once carried over $60,000 in student debt or Tim (who wrote the Afterword of this book) and LeAnn Norris who had over $400,000 in student loans. All three of them made monumental sacrifices to pay off that debt. Yet many others in similar situations find themselves struggling to repay their student loans.

Imagine a world where the government was committed to financial literacy as well as wellness and invested more in helping families make smarter college choices. What if our society spent more money, time, and attention on addressing the student loan crisis by educating students before they take on the debt? Well...until then, you have this book!

Within these pages you will read about how I was able to earn a bachelor's and master's degree from a reputable university completely debt free. Additionally, I've included other stories from individuals who also said no to student loan debt during their college days. The point of these stories is to share with you that *IT IS POSSIBLE* to earn a college degree and receive a diploma in the mail instead of invoices for student loans.

Fortunately, there are a lot of efforts underway to help people with student loans, including a growing number of employers that are committing themselves to financial wellness with college coaching and student debt repayment benefits. Let's alert young people about risk and reward and provide them with knowledge and tools to make informed decisions about their education and future employment. There are many different resources out there (see Resources section) that can help you pay your way through college.

So, how do we avoid student loan debt in the first place?

PART I

THE PROBLEM

THE STUDENT LOAN DEBT CRISIS

Student loan debt in America is the largest form of any debt,
other than home mortgages.

This just in—college is expensive. Over the past 45 years, gas prices have increased about 300%, gold has risen more than 1,200%, but the cost of college has outpaced them both skyrocketing more than 1,600% higher than it was in 1975. Undoubtedly, the extraordinary cost of college has resulted in more students feeling forced to take out student loans. Today nearly 70% of students take out loans to help pay for school. Now consider that 40% of attendees at a four-year college drop out before completing their degree. If you are part of that 40%, not only have you incurred some of the expense of college, you left without receiving a degree. For the 60% that do complete their degree, a whopping 64% take longer than four years to graduate, costing themselves nearly $70,000.

In an interview with CNN, Purdue University President and

former Governor of Indiana Mitch Daniels offered his thoughts on the student loan debt crisis:

The student debt system is the indentured servitude. You can't get away from it. You are stuck with that debt and can't even escape it in bankruptcy. It is burdening students long after their college years. We see people postponing homeownership, postponing marriage, and postponing families. The rate of new business formation from those who have borrowed money is quite naturally lower than others so it's hurting the economy in a variety of ways. The cost of college has risen faster than anything else in the economy. Faster than healthcare. Meanwhile, students have been encouraged to take on more and more loans to pay for diplomas which are sometimes, by the way, of suspect value to them in the marketplace. So, it's not been a good bargain for a lot of students. The federal government has been one of the drivers in raising the cost of college, which is the basic problem in the first place. If college didn't cost so much, students wouldn't be borrowing so much.

---

* * *

Drowning in Debt

Many young Americans are being crushed by school loan debt. While investing in yourself is usually wise, we must ask at what cost. Nearly 74% of first-generation students in the class of 2015-16 borrowed money for their undergraduate education. According to a study by the Consumer Federation of America (CFA), the average amount owed per federal student loan borrower stands at $34,000. That's up 62% over the last decade.

The CFA also found that millions of people had not made a payment on $137 billion in federal student loans for at least nine months in 2016, a 14% increase in defaults from a year earlier. The consumer watchdog (CFA) used the latest data from the Education Department, which manages nearly $1.7 trillion in federal student debt owed by 45 million Americans. And the repayment of that debt is one of the factors stalling our economy. If nothing changes, experts predict that by 2023, 40% of student borrowers will default on their loans and cause a recession.

World's Worst Dropout Rate

The United States has the worst college dropout rate of any developed country. Around 54% of first-generation students don't complete their degree. First-generation, low-income students had a six-year bachelor's degree completion rate of 21%. Students who are first-generation but not low-income still had a bachelor's degree completion rate of just 31%, according to data analyzed by the Pell Institute. Also consider that at most public universities, only 19% of full-time students earn a bachelor's degree in four years. In my home state of Georgia, it's estimated that more than 10,000 students drop out of colleges and universities every year because they simply can't afford the tuition.

* * *

Sara Goldrick-Rab wrote a fantastic book called *Paying the Price: College Costs, Financial Aid, and the Betrayal of the American Dream.* Her thoroughly researched book examines the broken college financial aid system that, in many cases, has done more harm to students than good. She says:

Despite its good intentions, our current financial aid system is failing today's students. When nearly 75% of American families find college unaffordable, and the means-tested financial aid system fails to do its job even for the poorest, it is time for a change.

Financial Aid 1.0 today is a pale shadow of what its creators intended. Rather than supporting the hopes and dreams of people who seek to study and get ahead through higher education, it is punitive. It acts as an enticement to try college but then sets up students to face prices they cannot afford to meet year after year. It pits students against parents, financial aid administrators, and each other. It makes those who end up short of funds feel as if they've done something wrong. It is an invitation to debt.

Student debt should not be at the center of this debate. Debt is the symptom, not the disease—the real problem is that college is unaffordable. Sixty percent of Americans aged 25 to 64 do not hold a college credential. But 22% of them—32.6 million Americans—have tried to get one. A year or two of college credits without a degree means not only wasted time but also significant debt.

Ultimately, we have to build a new system—a Financial Aid 2.0 that is based on accessible and affordable, high-quality, public, higher education.

What does all this mean? Most students enter college with the goal of earning a degree and boosting their prospects for a higher-paying job (dare I say *career*) after graduating. The reality is that many students are not finishing and are, instead, entering the work world with no degree and mounds of debt to deal with. Carrying massive debt—especially at a young age—

severely limits your future opportunities such as buying a home or being able to afford to raise children.

* * *

The Birth of a Crisis

In 1957 the Soviet Union launched the Sputnik satellite into orbit and beat America into space. Two months later the U.S. tried and failed to launch its own satellite. The U.S. feared that they were falling behind and the space race had begun. So, what does this have to do with student loan debt?

Then U.S. President Dwight Eisenhower was so embarrassed that he turned his focus on science and national security by giving high priority to scientific education. At the time, less than 8% of Americans had bachelor's degrees—mainly because many people couldn't afford it. Sound familiar? Student loans weren't really an option because banks weren't interested in handing out thousands of dollars to teenagers. As a result, in 1958, President Eisenhower signed the National Defense Education Act. It created the first federal loan program for students who were good at science, math, or engineering, and who promised not to try and violently overthrow the government. The bill allowed college students to borrow up to $1,000 a year from the federal government. Everyone hoped that these students would one day beat the Soviets in their scientific cold war.

A few years later, President Lyndon Johnson expanded the student loan program by signing the Higher Education Act of 1965. The act created a low-interest loan program for everyone —not just science nerds—and provided grants that didn't need to be paid back for low-income students. At the time, education costs were low and college enrollment grew along with the U.S. economy. As student loans helped more people go to college, the demand for higher education increased and so did the cost.

As a result, students took out bigger loans each year—especially after the government began cutting federal funding to public institutions.

In the late 1970s the widespread public backlash against high taxes that began in California contributed to Ronald Reagan's election to the White House in 1980. The revolt led to states passing tax and expenditure limitations, restrictions that state governments created to limit the amount they can tax or spend. Consequently, state budgets were threatened—meaning states that once highly subsidized college educations for many people started to cut back in various ways, either by raising tuition or by spending less. When Reagan cut higher education funding and student aid, you guessed it, college costs soared as a result.

The most recent major change in student loans came with the Student Aid and Fiscal Responsibility Act of 2009. Under this act, guaranteed loans were eliminated in 2010 and replaced with direct loans because of a belief that guaranteed loans benefited private student loan companies at taxpayers' expense. Basically, the government took over the student loan industry because lending money and keeping people in debt is BIG business in America. Prior to 2010, students had the option to choose a private-sector lender for their guaranteed loans. Now they only have one choice—the government. Banks can continue to make private, non-guaranteed college loans, but these are generally more expensive than guaranteed loans. Of course, none of these changes reduced the costs for the students.

To summarize, we are in a student loan debt crisis because our country was humiliated when another country launched a rocket into space before us!

* * *

Real-Life Story: Student Loan Thoughts from a Friend

My friend David Lee Windecher is one of the most interesting and unique individuals I've known. After spending a significant amount of his childhood in Argentina, a Third World country, David's family moved to North Miami Beach, Florida. There, he was an impoverished minority who was arrested 13 times and spent more than seven months incarcerated as a juvenile. He dropped out of high school and joined a criminal street gang in an attempt to overcome his poverty-stricken life.

Through a series of events that included encouragement from several influential people who entered his life, David began his path to rehabilitation when he received his GED and took his first academic step toward becoming a dual-licensed practitioner. With God's grace and sheer determination, David conquered his past to become a criminal defense attorney licensed to practice in Georgia and Florida. However, his journey came at an astounding cost. As a result of David's criminal history, his law school application was rejected by 39 out of the 40 schools he applied to. After being accepted to Atlanta's private, for-profit, John Marshall Law School, David racked up over $300,000 in student loan debt by the time he graduated. David chronicled his miraculous journey of transitioning from defendant to defense attorney in his inspirational autobiography, *The AmerIcan Dream | HisStory In The Making.*

I asked David for some of his thoughts specifically regarding student loans. Here's what he said:

My book has always been a positive thing. I didn't want to put anything [student loans] in there because I didn't want people to feel dissuaded from seeing the debt I incurred. I obviously accomplished more than I ever imagined and dreamed of because I was able to take on that debt.

America cannot meet the demands of the future by employing strategies of the past. We must evolve, starting with the cost of education. Growing up, kids are taught that going to school, continuing on to college, and working hard after receiving a degree guarantees a job and success. The reality is far different. Without parents who can write the tuition check and without scholarships, most students turn to loans, which is a grave mistake.

Sallie Mae, the largest student loan company in America, owns Pioneer Credit Recovery—and I don't mean "credit recovery" as in when your credit is poor they assist in rebuilding it. Yes, the largest student loan company in America also owns one of the collection agencies employed by the education department to collect student loan payments. Coincidence? Absolutely not!

Tuition lenders know borrowers will default. They charge you administrative fees to procure the loans. They charge you interest over the life of the loan which compounds as the balance grows. They defer payments while you're in school to create the illusion that it's feasible to earn an education while not paying. Yet, they charge you interest which increases your balance exponentially. Then they make you believe they are doing you a favor by allowing you to defer payments for the first 12 months after graduation, so you can focus on establishing a career. Of course, the interest continues to accumulate. When it is time to repay, the terms are never favorable. If you miss one payment, they will report you to collection agencies (which, as it turns out, is as simple as sending an email to the department one floor up). Once you are in collections, they threaten to take everything away. And they actually do by garnishing your pay for the next 30 years. These companies are setting people up to fail.

You need to accept that the American education system is designed and operated solely to earn lenders a profit. I'm sorry to say that your government is betting on your failure. When you fail, they win. Incurring massive amounts of educational debt is just another form of imprisonment.

The Department of Education is really taking advantage of people because people use academics as a safety net. They know they get some kind of funds to survive to cover their expenses. And people make a mistake because they don't have a vision, and if you don't have a vision, you are going to lose big time. If you can't see the invisible, you'll never create the impossible. So, you have to have a bigger vision for yourself before you can take on this kind of money [debt]. I had a vision, and do I still owe money? Absolutely, but I'm still in the process of unfolding my plan. It's sad to think about these things, but the reality is, if you don't have a vision for why you are taking on this kind of debt, it may not be a good investment.

Despite being saddled with an enormous amount of student loan debt, David has worked extremely hard since earning his law degree to become a successful attorney, author, and activist. Additionally, he founded RED Inc., which stands for Rehabilitation Enables Dreams. The nonprofit's mission is to eliminate the recidivism of America's marginalized youths by intervening at the onset of criminal behavior and building bridges to social advancement through education, support, and community partnerships.

David still holds a hefty balance on his student loan accounts but has diligently been paying it off with the goal of eliminating it completely in the near future.

* * *

Depression and Anxiety

Have you noticed in the news lately there's been an inordinate number of stories regarding college students and mental health? *Time* magazine published a feature titled, "Depression on Campus: Record numbers of college students are seeking treatment for depression and anxiety. Schools can't keep up." Students are facing the reality that a college degree is both more necessary and more expensive today than ever before—resulting in health concerns that university systems are not adequately staffed to manage. Could the exorbitant amount of student loan debt be a contributing factor?

Student Loan Debt = Divorce

Who didn't see this coming? Over time, the stress of carrying debt, in this case student loan debt, takes a toll on relationships. According to a study by Student Loan Hero, a website for managing education debt, more than a third of borrowers said college loans and other money factors contributed to their divorce. In fact, 13% of divorcees blamed student loans, specifically, for ending their relationship.

Changing Lifestyles

This situation alone has transformed how the millennial generation is living life. Many of them have moved back home with their parents after graduation and are waiting much longer to buy a house, get married, and have kids—if at all. One might deduce that this trend means another depressed economy is seemingly inevitable. But don't despair—there is hope and there is help.

Final Thoughts

Undoubtedly, the exorbitant cost of college has directly led to many students taking out massive loans that they are finding increasingly difficult to pay back. While investing in yourself is usually wise, we must ask at what cost. It's time to start critically evaluating the true value of a college education versus the return on investment. For example, if you want to become a restaurant owner, chef, or food truck operator, do you really need a four-year degree? Or can you accomplish the same goals by obtaining an apprenticeship or certificate-based training for a fraction of the cost? Chapter 11 (Alternatives to College) will cover this in greater detail, but I implore you to research all your options of obtaining further education and/or work-based training to pursue your passion.

2

THE REAL COST OF COLLEGE

*I learned law so well, the day I graduated I sued the college,
won the case, and got my tuition back.* - Fred Allen

I'm always amused when the media reports on how much
college will be in 18 years after a baby is born. Here's
some data I found in an article published by Market-
Watch in 2018: "It will cost today's newborns a whopping
$302,700 to attend a four-year private college in 2036, according
to a new calculation from the wealth-management company
Wealthfront. That's up from $166,800 today. If parents started
saving now, they would need to put away $980 per month for 18
years in a 529 plan, the report found. That assumes returns of
4% over 18 years."

I generally don't place a lot of value in these types of fear-
based reports. Perhaps these articles are trying to scare you into
saving and investing your money, I'm not sure. However, if
these figures were true it would prevent most Americans from
attending college.

The term "sticker shock" originated in auto dealership showrooms, but its new home is the admissions offices of colleges and universities. Schools have blurred the true cost of college by advertising prices that scare consumers and then discounting the price dramatically with a financial aid package that makes it feel like too good of a deal to pass up. For example, the advertised cost for attending Harvard University in 2017-2018 was $73,600, which would cause severe sticker shock to most families. While the *actual cost* for students who receive financial aid averages out to something closer to $12,000.

Standard College Expenses

In what should be a surprise to no one, the actual cost of a college degree is more than you might think. The following is a breakdown of all the expenses you can expect before earning that coveted degree:

- **Tuition and Fees** – This is what colleges charge for services that may include the library, campus transportation, student government, technology, and athletic facilities. They are rarely optional. In various college cost compilations, colleges often report a combined tuition and fees figure. According to College Board, the average tuition and fees combination for the 2017–2018 school year was $34,740 at private colleges, $9,970 for state residents at public colleges and $25,620 for out-of-state residents who attended public universities.

- **Housing and Meals** – Also described as "room and board," this line item depends on which campus housing and food plans you choose. College Board reported a range of average room and board in 2017–

2018 from $10,800 at four-year public schools to $12,210 at private schools. Schools typically provide an estimated cost of living off campus at schools where that is allowed.

- **Books and School Supplies** – Based on college cost estimates for required learning materials (sometimes including the cost of purchasing a laptop), College Board reported the average cost for books and supplies for the 2017–2018 school year was $1,250 at public colleges and $1,220 at private colleges.

- **Personal and Transportation Expenses** – Colleges may also provide estimates for attendance-related expenses that will never show up on bills that come directly from the school. These costs include local transportation, clothing, personal items, and entertainment. Don't forget that campus parking permits may come with a hefty price tag. Parking permits at Louisiana State University cost $165 per year, or $80 for a semester only. Parking permits for Ohio State University range from $109.20 to $887.76 annually. The College Board reported expenses in this category for 2017–2018 ran from $2,730 at private colleges to $3,270 at public universities.

TOTAL: Going by the above data, the total cost to attend a public college as an in-state student would be $25,290 per year and $101,160 after four years.

Hidden College Expenses
Tuition, along with the other aforementioned items, aren't

the only expenses when it comes to a college education. The following represents further costs that could prove unexpected for many families—some occur prior to arriving on campus.

- **Application Fees** – Individual application fees usually aren't prohibitively expensive. However, if you apply to enough schools, they can add up quickly. For example, if you are shelling out $40 or $50 to apply for college it may not seem like much, but if you are casting your net wide enough and apply to multiple schools the expenses can rapidly mount. On average, top-ranked schools charge anywhere from $75 to $90 to apply. If a student is applying to seven schools, that can add up to somewhere between $525 and $630—not an insignificant cost.

- **Club and Organization Fees** – Socializing comes at a price in college. Many club memberships require fees or additional expenses, and Greek life tends to be the most expensive. Campus organizations often charge membership dues ($10-$25 at the low end), but it can get much more costly for students looking to join a sorority or fraternity. UCLA estimates the average annual cost of room, board, and dues to be about $7,650 for sororities and $8,328 for fraternities. That's before adding in all the other membership costs like clothing and fees to attend social functions. Interested in joining a club sport? Dues can run as much as $2,500 per year, according to the Texas A&M Department of Recreational Sports.

- **Furniture and Décor** – Plan to budget several hundred dollars for furniture and décor. If you're lucky, your dorm or apartment might include a few pieces of furniture. However, you'll still need bedding, curtains, linens, among other staples. The good news is that any college town where students are constantly moving in and leaving each year is great for the reseller's market. Check out Craigslist in your area to save on furniture, or resale sites like AptDeco or Furnishly. Social media sites like Facebook marketplace and Nextdoor classifieds (for sale and free) are also good places to find deals.

- **Traveling to and from Home** – How many times each year will students return home from college? On average, probably two such round-trips. Subsequently, how many times will parents visit their kids on campus? Perhaps once a year, on average. If you and your student are traveling by air, all those flights could easily add up to thousands in travel costs. But even if your child is road-tripping home, gas and tolls alone can cost hundreds annually—not to mention hotel costs when you visit campus.

- **Moving or Storing Your Stuff** – At the end of each school year, a college student will have three options: 1) remain near campus throughout the summer, 2) trek home with all his/her belongings in tow, or 3) return home after moving all the belongings into storage near campus. If your student stays near campus, budget at least several hundred dollars per month to sublease a room or a full apartment. Hauling your stuff home each summer will likely be a bit more expensive. U-Haul's rates vary by pickup location and the length of your rental. For example, a 10-foot, U-Haul truck used for an in-state move could cost about $125-250, fuel included. For a cross-country move of over 500 miles, it could cost $650 or more.

- **Studying Abroad and other Travel** – College years are prime time for travel. Whether you're hitting the beach with friends on spring break or considering an extended study abroad program, you could easily spend thousands of dollars on travel over the course of four years.Study abroad programs, complete with room, board, instruction, and sometimes internships, can get pricey. For example, Northwestern University estimates a year studying abroad in Brazil to cost about $21,000 for students, while a summer abroad in the University of Georgia's UGA en Buenos Aires program costs $4,294, plus about $3,000 in tuition and fees.

- **Internships** – An unpaid internship may mean forgoing income from summer employment. Even if the internship is paid, you may have high costs for living expenses, depending on the location of the internship.

- **Sports Tickets** – At many schools, attending on-campus football or basketball games is a vital part of the college experience—and maybe even a reason why your son or daughter chose to attend a particular college. Although students generally get a large discount, season tickets for football alone can range from $72 (Virginia Tech) to $245 (Notre Dame). Student season tickets to both basketball and football games at Indiana University are $390. If your child's school is a powerhouse at a popular sport, expect tickets to be more expensive for that set of games.

- **Health Insurance and Medical Costs** – If students do not have health coverage through their parents, some schools may require you to sign up for a health plan. For example, New York University automatically enrolls students in its school-sponsored healthcare plan, but students can waive the plan if they can provide documentation they maintain alternate health insurance coverage that meets the university's minimum health insurance criteria. The cost of a basic plan for the spring 2017 semester: $1,654. If you're an out-of-state student and don't find alternative insurance coverage in time for classes, you could be stuck paying the bill as "NYU requires that all students registered in degree-granting programs maintain health insurance."

* * *

Other Factors to Consider

Changing Majors – If you switch majors, you might have to take extra classes to get on track with your new major. This can add a semester or two of extra college costs before you can graduate. Do your research to gain an idea of what extra costs you might incur.

Time in School – The time you spend in school can also drive up the total cost of your degree. Most estimates—for tuition, room and board, and other expenses—assume four years in college, the time most students expect to spend getting a bachelor's degree. However, the reality is that many students end up in school far longer which accumulates more costs. In fact, according to the National Center for Education Statistics' most recent data, only 39.4% of first-time undergraduate students at four-year colleges actually graduate in four years, and 59% graduate in six years.

It took me nearly six years to get my four-year bachelor's and three years to earn my two-year master's.

Yearly Increase of Costs – This is a factor that many of us don't take into account. When you are calculating your annual college expenses, most of us will simply add up all the costs for the first year then multiple it by four. Unfortunately, this is not entirely accurate. First, as previously mentioned, most students do not graduate within four years—so you will need to factor the potential cost of extra years in school.

Perhaps more importantly, the cost of tuition as well as expenses generally increase yearly. On average, tuition tends to increase about 8% per year. An 8% college inflation rate means that the cost of college doubles every nine years. For a baby born today, this means that college costs will be more than three times current rates when the child matriculates in college. Additionally, you must factor in the average annual rate of inflation in the U.S. is around 2-3%, which will drive up the cost of your other living expenses.

Is It Worth It?

College is expensive and prohibitively so for many students. That doesn't necessarily mean it isn't worth it. As studies show, college degrees still lead to greater employment opportunities, higher wages, and even, some say, better health. However, it's important to consider the return on investment you're getting from your education—an issue experts in the higher education space are considering, too.

According to a recent Gallup report, only half of college students feel strongly that their education was worth the cost. Recent college graduates were less likely to think their education was worth it, as were graduates of for-profit colleges.

Ultimately, it's up to individual students and their families to determine how much they can and want to spend on college, and to ensure they're getting a return on their investment. However, there are many ways to lower the cost of college from scholarships to simple budgeting. Until something changes in the world of higher education, students and families are going to have to continue to rely on a variety of resources to help pay for college and keep student debt at a minimum.

* * *

DID YOU KNOW?

- Only 27% of college graduates work in a field related to their major.
- 41% of recent college graduates work in jobs not requiring a degree.

Source: Study from the Federal Reserve Bank of New York.

* * *

Final Thoughts

Whew. Writing this chapter gave me serious sticker shock along with anxiety of how much college is going to eventually cost for my 5-year-old and 1-year-old sons. As you can see, the costs of college have gotten out of control, which has forced many people into massive amounts of student loan debt—a vicious cycle that seems to be getting worse. But I'm here to tell you that there is another way. There are alternatives to walking across the stage to get your diploma along with a payment plan for $40,000 of student loan debt.

It's time to start seriously evaluating the major you choose and courses you select. Research the job market. Find out where and what the growing jobs are along with the in-demand skill sets. Meet with advisors, counselors, and career coaches to discover what the average starting salaries are in the industry you are passionate about. If you have a heart for serving others and desire to work in the nonprofit industry, that's great, but you might be making $30,000 a year. So, you need to take that into account before you accept a large amount of loans. How long will it take for you to pay it back making a salary of $X, etc.? I've heard many stories from people who thought they would only need about $10,000 worth of loans to get through college and it ended up being $80,000. Don't let this be you!

PART II

THE STORIES

3

HOW I EARNED A DEBT-FREE BACHELOR'S DEGREE

I'm a great believer in luck, and I find the harder I work the more I have of it. - Thomas Jefferson

The path that led to my potential college options (or lack thereof) began in the summer of 1990 when I turned 15. Entering my sophomore year of high school, I was now legally of age to work. As a result, my parents informed me that anything I wanted to buy was my responsibility to pay for. Like most teenagers, I coveted a car, so I began work immediately as a courtesy clerk (bagger) at Kroger. Earning the minimum wage of $3.80 an hour and being limited to 15 hours a week due to child labor laws would prove difficult to save money for a car, much less college. While attending high school in Marietta, Georgia, most of my classmates boasted their plans of attending the University of Georgia while some had aspirations of enrolling at Georgia Tech. Due to my grades, SAT scores, and financial means, I had no chance of attending such prestigious schools. My opportunities were greatly limited, which turned out to be a blessing in disguise.

The Journey Begins

The fall of 1993 was the beginning of my collegiate journey at Kennesaw State University (KSU) located in Kennesaw, Georgia—just north of Atlanta. It was the only school I applied to because it was my *only* chance of obtaining a higher education. Back then, it was known as Kennesaw State College and was a commuter school with an enrollment of about 13,000. [KSU's enrollment is now more than 41,000.] Although I had been working since my 15th birthday, there was no college savings, nor were my parents in a financial position to assist me. Therefore, living at home and commuting to school was my *only* option in order to pay my way through.

During the start of my college career, I was a part-time employee of Chick-fil-A—working full-time hours making $5.25 an hour. With my parents graciously letting me live at home for free, most of my money was used on school, transportation, and fast food. After two years at Chick-fil-A, the company awarded me a $1,000 scholarship. Back then, KSU was on the quarter system, so that paid for almost two quarters and was a huge help. At the time, I believe tuition was about $550 per quarter—a far cry from today's rates. Out of convenience, I quit Chick-fil-A to find work closer to campus. After landing a retail job at Town Center Mall in Kennesaw about a mile away, I became more involved in on-campus activities— joining the staff of *The Sentinel* (KSU's student newspaper) as a sports writer/editor as well as working in the sports information department within the athletic department. Back then my passion for sports was leading me toward becoming a sports broadcaster.

. . .

Working to Prevent Debt

As a junior, I was working three jobs and going to school full time. The jobs were ideal because two of them were on campus and the mall job was across the street. Even with three jobs, money was not plentiful. At the mall, I worked for a store called Sports Fantasy that sold team apparel and novelties. Despite earning around $6.50 an hour, my fortunes changed due to the company going out of business. I was bummed to lose a cool job that allowed me to hang out with my friends. (Did I mention there was an arcade next door?) As a result of recently being promoted to the store's assistant manager, I qualified to receive a severance package that included a lump sum payment of $2,000. At 21, it was easily the most money I'd ever seen, and the amount would cover another year of my schooling.

After being promoted to sports editor, my job at *The Sentinel* paid $50 a week, and KSU Athletics paid me as a game worker. Operating scoreboards, keeping statistics, and serving as the public-address announcer for various sports were some of the tasks I performed. Athletics paid me $10 to $15 a game—depending on the sport. I basically worked as a volunteer within the sports information office, although I did turn that work into an internship course credit and which also helped me gain valuable experience.

During my junior year the athletic department rewarded me with a book scholarship that compensated me for all my materials for one academic year. Entering the fall quarter, I was notified that I had been selected to serve as a communications intern at ESPN—The Worldwide Leader in Sports. The prominent sports, cable-TV station was headquartered in Bristol, Connecticut. It was a full-time, 40-hour a week position that paid $6.50 an hour. I moved to Bristol and rented a room from a homeowner who lived near the station. The internship was 17 weeks and all the money I made was used to live a very frugal lifestyle. The term "starving intern" definitely applied to me during this time.

The Game Changer

After the Christmas and New Year's holiday break, I returned to finish my degree at KSU and was blessed with more good fortune when then-Athletic Director Dr. Dave Waples changed my life. Perhaps feeling guilty for all the uncompensated hours I'd poured into Owls' Athletics over the previous three years, Dr. Waples put me on a full *athletic scholarship* for my final year of school. To my knowledge, I was the first *non-athlete* to receive an athletic scholarship. It completely covered my tuition and books. Dr. Waples and his generosity proved pivotal in my journey.

On August 8, 1998, (Yes, it took me nearly six years!) I graduated with a bachelor's degree in media communication and walked across the stage completely debt free—naïve to the fact of my massive accomplishment. My grades weren't spectacular (2.7 GPA), possibly due to working all those jobs, but never did it occur to me to take out student loans. That was not part of my mindset. Perhaps because my parents never modeled or preached that debt is the answer. If you don't have the cash to pay for it, you can't do it. That's what I've always thought. So, what do you do when you live that mantra? You find a way to get the cash. You work hard and become resourceful and creative. I recognize that the cost of college has ballooned since my undergrad days and many students feel forced into loans (or feel that debt is a way of life) in order to earn their degrees. There is another way! Do whatever you can do to either graduate debt free or limit the loans you incur. Your 35-year-old self will be forever thankful. Trust me.

Receiving my degree from the late Dr. Betty Siegel.

How I Earned My Bachelor's Degree Debt Free

- Attended an in-state college
- Lived at home
- Worked several jobs (on and off campus)
- Earned scholarship money
- Bought used books

4

HOW I EARNED A DEBT-FREE MASTER'S DEGREE

Opportunity is missed by most people because it is dressed in overalls and looks like work. - Thomas Edison

In the fall of 2013, I came home to work full time for my alma mater as the first and sole copywriter for KSU's College of Professional Education. A highlighted benefits perk was the opportunity to further my education for free. The school offered a Tuition Assistance Program (TAP) that would cover all tuition costs of any degree program. My out-of-pocket expenses would be for books and any other incidentals. The only caveat would be that I'd have to be employed for six months before I would be eligible to apply for the assistance.

The lone program KSU offered that interested me was its Master of Arts in Professional Writing (MAPW). Realizing the regret would be greater if I didn't go for it, I began the application process. Never in my wildest dreams did I think: 1) I would even qualify for grad school (see undergrad GPA in previous chapter); and 2) I would ever be going back to school—especially at my age. Just the words *grad school* were very intimidating after being out of school for 15 years.

Grad School Prep

The next year was spent preparing for the GRE (graduate records examination) and working on the arduous application requirements. The process was very similar to applying for a high-profile job. Several influential people wrote letters of recommendation on my behalf which helped tremendously. An enormous relief was felt when the acceptance letter arrived in the fall of 2015 and my status as "student" began in January 2016. The best advice I received was from the program director who said to start with just one class in order to "ease into the grad-life experience." I'm glad I listened because it was a radical change in lifestyle.

Major Life Changes

Working at KSU during the day and going to grad school at night comprised the next three years of my life. Adding to the challenge was the birth of our first child during my first semester of school. (He granted my request and arrived during spring break, which resulted in not missing any classes.) After completing only one class my first semester, I plugged away taking two classes at a time (which was considered full time) to set me on a track to graduate within three years.

Although 100% of my tuition was being paid for by KSU, I was still responsible for acquiring my own books and supplies. To save money, most of my books were purchased in used condition on Amazon or eBay. One difference in book usage that didn't exist during my undergrad days was the option to rent. However, after much research I discovered that most rental rates were about the same cost as it would be to buy a used book. In most cases, it made sense to buy and own the book then sell it and hope to recoup at least half of my money. Being a professional writing student required an inordinate amount of reading. On average, most of my classes required at least three books. However, I remember being astonished at needing seven books for my technical writing class. Fortunately, I unearthed some small scholarship opportunities that I qualified for.

Securing Scholarships

Since my employer, KSU's College of Professional Education was a member of the Association for Continuing Higher Education (ACHE), I was eligible to apply for its regional Joseph P. Goddard Scholarship Award. The $1,000 scholarship is presented to adult students (25 years of age or older) who are engaged in studies in an accredited graduate degree program. Since I checked all those boxes I applied and was blessed to be selected for the award. Additionally, KSU offered annual scholarship awards of $500 to employees who were also furthering their education at the school. The first year I applied the selection committee did not call my name. However, I didn't give up and applied again the following year. To my surprise, my name was announced at the awards ceremony in front of all my peers. In total, I received $1,500 which I applied toward book purchases. Due to my thrifty book shopping, I did not spend anywhere close to $1,500 and actually made money from going to grad school—a far cry from many of my classmates who were already $80,000 in debt from their undergrad loans and piling on more debt at a rapid pace.

Many people may feel intimated by the scholarship application process or think it takes an inordinate amount of time. However, this was not the case in my experience. In fact, there's so much unclaimed scholarship money out there—you simply have to do your research and know where to look. Case in point: when I was an employee of KSU, our College of Professional Education had hundreds of thousands of dollars in scholarship money available that was never used. Why? Most likely it's a result of three things—1) people don't know the opportunities are available; 2) people think they will not qualify and don't even bother to apply; or 3) people are scared away by the perceived competition for the award.

I'm willing to bet that the $1,000 scholarship I received was because I was the only person who applied for it. Maybe others thought that $1,000 was not enough money to help them so they didn't even bother. Not me. Any financial help was beneficial. Both scholarship applications I won required me to write around a 250-word essay describing why I had selected my course of studies and how the money would help me achieve my goals. The essay topics were open-ended allowing me to have a range of discussion. The little time I spent on the application process and writing the essays versus the amount of money I received was well worth it.

New Job. New Benefits.

During the summer of 2018 a job offer was presented to me that I could not refuse—a copywriter/copyeditor position for HNTB, a transportation consulting firm in Atlanta. Sadly, this meant losing out on any remaining TAP money from KSU, but luckily only one semester remained to be paid for. In preparation to cough up the nearly $3,000 for my final semester, I was pleasantly surprised to discover my new employer offered a tuition reimbursement program. Fortunately, there was no waiting period, so I couldn't apply fast enough. HNTB's program was different in that it was a *reimbursement* so I had to front the money for my tuition. In order to receive my tuition money back from my new employer, I would have to submit my final grades after the semester along with all documented receipts, etc. This situation resulted in our family having to do some creative budgeting to manage the large expense initially coming out of our pocket.

On December 11, 2018, I graduated completely debt free with a Master of Arts in Professional Writing (a degree valued at nearly $20,000) from Kennesaw State University. It was a massive relief on so many different levels. Many people supported me through this three-year journey—especially my wife who sacrificed a great deal in caretaking for our newborn son. I felt fortunate and blessed to have successfully, as well as resourcefully, found a way to earn an advanced degree during the student loan debt crisis era.

What a relief! Celebrating my master's degree with my wife Amethyst and son Maddux. WE DID IT!

How I Earned My Master's Degree Debt Free

- Worked for the university where I attended school and received a full tuition waiver
- Earned scholarship money
- Qualified for employer tuition reimbursement program (after leaving university job)
- Bought used books (renting books can now be a cheaper option in some cases)

General Tips to Avoid Student Loans

- Attend an in-state school
- Work while in school
- Look for jobs that offer employer-based tuition coverage
- Seek on-campus jobs that may offer tuition waiver and stipends
- Apply for every scholarship you're eligible for

I hope you can see from my stories that *YOU CAN* earn a college degree debt free and not have tens of thousands of dollars in debt hanging over your head for decades to come. If my stories aren't enough to convince you, check out the incredible stories from my friends in the next four chapters!

5

KATHERINE HUNT

*I graduated debt free with honors during a pandemic so it can
be done!*

I t's been said that God is the ultimate networker—or
connector in life. This couldn't be more true in how I
become connected to Katherine Hunt. However, some
might say it's total random luck.

My wife was grocery shopping at Kroger by herself with our
two young boys. As she was struggling to load everything into
our car along with the kids, Katherine's mom Sarah came
across the parking lot to help. A conversation was had and
somehow my wife brought up the fact that I was working on a
book about earning college degrees debt free. Sarah mentioned
that she has six grown kids and none of them have student loan
debt. As you might imagine, I perked up and immediately
contacted Sarah who then put me in touch with her daughter
Katherine.

There are many ways to pay for school in order to graduate

debt free. Katherine Hunt is a perfect example. At the time of our interview Katherine was 28 years old, single, with no kids, and living in Marietta, Georgia. She earned a bachelor's degree from Georgia State University in 2014 before claiming a juris doctorate degree from the school's College of Law in 2020. When Katherine yelled "I did it!" while walking across the stage, she was not only referring to earning her degrees but also accomplishing the feats debt free! How did she do it? Here is her story:

What is your view toward money? Did your parents (or anyone else) teach you about money when you were young?

With regard to money, I try to save as much as possible and avoid debt. I also spend a lot of money on things that matter to me (i.e. my fitness, gifts for others, and traveling) while I try to spend almost no money on things that do not matter to me (I get my hair cut at Great Clips). My parents consistently taught me to avoid debt when I was growing up, so it is almost second nature now. When I graduated college, I briefly worked in financial planning where I learned about investing so now that is important to me as well. My parents also taught me about good debt and some strategies for getting a good credit score. For instance, I opened a credit card account shortly after college and used it for small purchases just so I could pay it off every month. I also bought a car primarily with cash but financed a small portion so I could establish another payment history. Now I have a perfect credit score thanks to that advice.

Did you graduate college debt free? If so, share your story. How did you do it?

Yes, I did. I was lucky enough to receive the HOPE Scholarship which covered a majority of in-state tuition in Georgia.

Therefore, I was only responsible for $1,000-$2,000 worth of fees per semester. I worked full time during college, so I was able to cover the cost of fees and textbooks with my salary.

Did you go through law school debt free? Share how.

Yes. When I was accepted at Georgia State University College of Law, they offered me a merit scholarship of $4,000 per year. At the same time, I received a full scholarship from a private law school in another state. The guy I was dating at the time encouraged me to reach out to Georgia State (since it was my number one choice and alma mater) and ask that they reconsider the scholarship offer because I received a better offer from another school. I did, and they offered me $4,000 for my first year with a full scholarship and $4,000/year stipend for the following three years in exchange for me being a graduate research assistant. So, my dad and I paid for the balance of my first-year tuition out of pocket and I was essentially paid to go to school after that. In addition, the graduate research requirement enabled me to be an assistant to one of the deans of the law school, which was one of my favorite experiences in my entire education. She is now an esteemed close friend and an amazing reference and business connection.

What challenges did you face paying your way through schooling?

I worked full time through undergraduate education and law school, and it was exhausting at times. Oftentimes during law school, I felt stretched very thin between school, work, and my graduate research position and that was frustrating. However, my employer was very understanding of my class schedule and even let me take day classes during my third and fourth years of school. (I started as an evening student.) Ultimately, I graduated debt free with honors during a pandemic so it can be done!

Looking back, is there anything you would've done differently regarding how you managed money during your college years?

No. I did not make a lot of money during college, but I believe I spent and saved what I had wisely. Occasionally I probably spent too much money on something unnecessary like a trip, a fancy dinner, or clothes that I did not need but I don't regret that because sometimes you need to treat yourself! In my opinion, life is short and your budget should not make you miserable. Also, the lean years made me appreciate my current financial situation. Sometimes I find myself sitting in my dream car thinking how shocked my college self would be.

What are your thoughts on the student loan debt crisis?

I think it is very sad because a lot of people see debt as their only way to get a college education and that is certainly what they tell you at orientation. Part of my college orientation was a meeting with a school loan officer. They showed me three options and asked if I wanted to circle one and start paperwork. Thankfully, my dad was there to stop me because I thought you had to choose one.

Share your thoughts on the notion that "Education is 'good debt' because you are investing in yourself." Yet, people are leaving school (some not even graduating) with debt in the six figures.

I tend to disagree with this statement because education is probably not a good debt unless it results in an immediate six-figure salary. For some specialized professions (i.e. doctor, lawyer), debt is almost unavoidable. However, I think the best way to invest in yourself is by working and saving to pay for your desired level of education.

What advice would you give to students entering college regarding how to avoid student loan debt?

I always advise people to walk into financial aid and say, "I don't want loans—what else can I do?" I think a lot of people think that you must choose a lame community college OR get a loan to go to the cool state universities or private schools. That is not the case! Every school has so many scholarship opportunities and resources beyond merit-based scholarships. If you start early, you can create your own plan to finance your education through scholarships and grants. I also recommend getting a part-time job whether you need it for school or not. In my experience, employers are very eager to hire college graduates who already have experience in the workforce especially if they gained this experience while excelling in school.

6

THOMAS BUTTERWORTH

My grandfather always taught me "Don't take out loans for money you don't need."

Thomas Butterworth's wife and my wife met and became friends during their days as students together at Kennesaw State University. I met Thomas a few times briefly at various gatherings. After reading my first book, *Margin Matters: How to Live on a Simple Budget & Crush Debt Forever*, Thomas sent me an encouraging email with positive feedback. Within our subsequent conversations I discovered that he earned not one, but two debt-free degrees. Naturally I informed Thomas of this book project and asked him to share his story.

Having lived in Woodstock, Georgia, his entire life, Thomas is now 35, married 10 years, and has two beautiful daughters ages 5 and 3. In 2011 he earned a Bachelor of Science in Accounting at Southern Polytechnic State University—now Kennesaw State University (KSU). In 2018 he claimed his MBA with a certification in ethical leadership from KSU. Thomas is currently working in the oil industry as a senior information technology auditor for Colonial Pipeline.

What is your view toward money? Did your parents (or anyone else) teach you about money when you were young?

When I was growing up, I had no concept of money and how it impacted your life, nor did I have anyone giving me guidance on money. My parents tried to shield me from reality at times and they also created a world where I didn't understand the concept of money. Both my parents worked hard and came from challenging environments. They struggled, so when I was younger I think they were both learning [about money] themselves.

As I got into high school and started working part-time jobs, my parents mentioned opening accounts to put money into. They didn't teach me any concepts or justifications as to why we were doing these things (this was all prior to the days of the internet where you could just look things up for advice), so I would have to get information out of books—which I did not read. My grandparents were more influential as I got into high school, college, and into my young adult life giving me guidance because they both grew up at the end of the Great Depression. Therefore, they had more insight and struggle from where they came from.

To my view on money, I really didn't have a concept of what money was and how it can impact lives. Growing up, I did hear my parents having intense discussions about money. They had separate accounts, so I remember them saying, "I thought *you* were paying this bill?" "I thought *you* were paying that bill?" There was no sitting down and talking through all the bills.

. . .

Share the story of your progression from high school to college and how you graduated debt free?

It wasn't until my senior year of high school when I started applying for colleges and had no idea what my options were. There was no education or awareness, at least not in the high school that I went to. Everyone was going to college for the most part. I'd say about 90% of my high school class went to college.

My parents were banking on the [Georgia] HOPE Scholarship. That's what I was hoping for. At the time you had to maintain a 3.0 GPA and HOPE would cover the majority of tuition, books, and some of your housing. That was the go-to at the time—the HOPE Scholarship because of the cost. This was in 2004 and back then college was much more affordable than it is now.

The original plan was my parents and grandparents would assist with any costs not covered by HOPE. I also wanted to live on campus. My parents helped me out my first year. We had a deal in place, but I broke the deal, so I lost their financial support. I lost HOPE eventually. Not understanding truly how fortunate I was to have all that. That's the embarrassing part of the story. I had something so valuable that someone was willing to pay for the costs. I had the HOPE Scholarship to where I just flushed it down the toilet. I was definitely not in a mature state of mind at the time. I was not mature enough to go to college but because that was the track everyone was supposed to go down, everyone was rushed into it. That paved the way into why I had to adapt and adjust into having to pay for college myself.

What challenges did you face paying your way through schooling?

I ended up getting several part-time jobs putting in over 40 hours a week in multiple locations. I was working as a lab technician for a dentist office and as a telecom specialist for a telecommunications company. They allowed me to be extremely flexible. Another thing I did on the side was house sitting. Not only was I able to work these part-time jobs and go to school, but in the afternoons and evenings I housesat for individuals and got paid a daily rate. That subsidized my ability to pay for college.

While I started out with the HOPE Scholarship, I eventually lost it. So, I had to become extremely creative and realized that I had to pay for this. In the process I changed majors after doing a self-reflection and realized the degree program I was in, I loved as a hobby but hated as a career. This was also during the time of the Great Recession.

At one point I got laid off from one of my part-time positions, but I was able to pick up another one. That was how I was able to subsidize but it also took me seven years to finish, which encompasses my change in degrees from start to finish. I was one year away from graduating with my first degree and realized, "I just don't want to do this anymore." That was a tough pill to swallow. My parents and family were not excited about that decision. I decided, "I'm not happy in this. I just don't want to do it for the rest of my life." I'm very glad I made the change and did that self-reflection.

So that's the path I took—working those part-time jobs. Eventually while in school pursuing my undergraduate degree, I was offered a full-time position at the telecommunications company I was with. That [additional income] allowed me to pay for my schooling during that time as well.

Did you ever consider getting student loans?

In reality that's the thing [loans] that everyone goes to. I met with the financial services people from my school and they advised me on student loans. I was not going to go to my parents and ask them for money—I would've felt embarrassed doing that. "Hey, I've potentially failed at what I want to do. Can you help me in this situation?" My parents wouldn't cosign with me on any student loans, so I was very concerned with doing it. Yes, I could have taken out this money but how was I also going to be able to afford to live on campus?

I did work as a resident advisor for a while to be able to live on campus, but I didn't receive a paycheck from that role. I had to find ways to be able to pay for things. Yes, loans were an option but a lot of them were unsubsidized which would start gaining interest the time you take them out. Some of them were subsidized and I think we all need more education on knowing the differences between the two loans options. My grandfather always taught me "Don't take out loans for money you don't need." Our society, this was taught into us—everyone needs a credit card, student loans, mortgages. Those are just things you do.

I saw student loans as an option but because I realized that if I sacrificed in the short term, in the long term I wouldn't be paying for 10 to 20 years on the debt. Fortunately, because of the cost of the degrees at the time, I was able to have that money. I eventually moved back home to my parents' house— they welcomed me back, thankfully. The deal was as long as I was in school they would allow me to stay with them and provide me meals, but once I was done with school I had to move out or pay them rent. On the degree side, I realized I was able to pay for them and if I sacrificed a little more I wouldn't have to take out student loans. Although they were an option for me, thankfully I did not take out any student loans.

How did you avoid student loans to earn your MBA debt free?

For this degree I had less stress financially. I can't emphasis enough that if you work for a company that offers any type of tuition reimbursement, harness that to its fullest extent. That's what I did. I worked for a company that not only had a tuition reimbursement program, but also had no time requirement for that agreement. Some companies may reimburse you for tuition costs but expect a year of employment after that or else you would owe the taxes or the reimbursement back. That's how I was able to do it.

I was working a full-time job and around 2016 I started my master's program. Thankfully the two places where I worked during the time of earning my master's offered a tuition reimbursement program. I was able to earn my MBA completely debt free by harnessing both of those programs while using my personal funds to buy books. I used Chegg and Amazon to save money on books. You can also look for virtual books to save money. Professors seem to be pretty accepting of helping you find other options instead of buying a book for $350.

It took me a little longer to graduate—about 2.5 years in the program. My wife and I sacrificed on the things we would normally do to be able to afford this degree. We still had to live, but we figured out what we could do to cut costs.

Looking back, is there anything you would've done differently regarding how you managed money during your college years?

Yes, there is much that I would change. That being said, I also learned a lot during my financial struggles at this time in my life. I guess I could say I wish I had *known* things versus *done* things differently. Knowing would have allowed me to change more.

I would have kept the agreement with my parents and I would have kept the HOPE Scholarship. At that time in my life,

I did not understand how fortunate I was and the opportunities that I had. I wish I had not let my family down from a few choices, but that also helped me deal with failure and having to figure things out. I would have also pushed back on my parents for at least a year of working versus going to college. I felt pressured on a few levels to go to college even when I knew I was not ready. I also do not know what may have come of my life if I had chosen that path. My parents were concerned that I would not actually go to college, similar to their choices. Additionally, I would have looked for more scholarships after losing the HOPE Scholarship. I did not realize how many companies and other areas there are to get scholarships or non-commitment financial assistance.

One of the biggest challenges of being in school is the unspoken peer pressure of, "You should graduate in four to five years." I dealt with that personally because I saw a lot of my friends graduating from college [before me] and being successful. You are comparing yourself to other individuals. Looking back, I didn't choose to take out loans to potentially expedite how quickly I'd graduate. There were times that I didn't take full loads. That's a part of the student loan game—"Hey, get out in four or five years, you don't have to work, you can dedicate your time [to school]."

Wanting to go on trips with my friends was a struggle. I had a lot of friends who traveled the world who were fortunate with different opportunities or used student loans to help with travel expenses. I would've loved to see and tour the world, especially being younger and single at the time. I did save up to go on more local trips.

Looking back, I don't know if I would have changed a lot because I learned a lot of lessons. I wish somebody would have sat me down and taught me the management of money. I had no idea how to handle money. Not only was I working to pay tuition and fees, I was also working to pay credit cards off.

Having access to more information at a younger age would've been ideal. However, I was the first one in my family to graduate from college, so no one had that experience. A lot of the life lessons I learned early on, I learned from the trials I had to go through. Determining what am I going to do and how am I going to do it—and trying to create the solutions.

What are your thoughts on the student loan debt crisis?

It's an unfortunate thing that we've gotten to. If we look at history—the mortgage crisis (mortgage bubble) and now the student loan crisis—I think we are uninformed on certain decision levels. I've had many conversations with individuals who didn't understand the difference between subsidized and unsubsidized, yet they were able to sign the agreements and not fully understand what they were getting into. I think there is more awareness now.

I think it is important for people to evaluate their situation. For example, think about what you want to do, what the job market is like (likelihood of getting job), how much someone in a position you are after really makes after taxes and other costs, and how much will the degree cost? We think about how much a degree costs, but schools have so many fees and charge a premium to live on campus and to eat on campus.

Look at Kennesaw State University for example, an undergraduate degree costs in state $3,774 for 15 hours of courses and fees. If you live on campus, one plan they have is $3,825 per semester and meal plan of $1,770. So that is more doubling the cost of just going to school. I recognize that not everyone has a place to stay besides campus housing but I recommend people live with family or friends to save on costs. Living on campus can be fun, but that is another $5,000 a semester. Kennesaw State is also one of the more affordable schools in Georgia. Look at other options, such as a local university to then transfer into a larger full degree program university.

Share your thoughts on the notion that "Education is 'good debt' because you are investing in yourself." Yet, people are leaving school (some not even graduating) with debt in the six figures.

I do agree with the statements of good or bad debt, but it also should be considered informed and uninformed debt. Yes, I think education is extremely important. I think continuous education and challenging yourself is very important. At the same time, I think there's a limit to the cost. Consider in-state versus out of state. Look at all your options. I have a friend who's taken out $90,000 for an undergraduate accounting degree. He says it will take him 20 years to pay it back. Do I believe there is good debt? I don't know if that's the best way to say it, but I think there are forms of debt that are necessary and others that are unnecessary—which I think is probably the majority.

I have another friend who bused to Atlanta every day when he was in college, worked a full-time job, and came back and went to school. It took him seven-and-a-half years to graduate college, but he graduated debt free. I respect him for that accomplishment. Not everyone has the patience or self-control for that.

Try to be as informed as you can. Many people don't want to talk about finances because it's personal and emotional. I encourage those to think about having a trusted relationship with someone to have those conversations. What are your struggles? Remember, these financial institutions make money off the interest! Think about all your options. Student debt has its place but there are definitely opportunities with companies to pay for your degree.

. . .

What advice would you give to students entering college regarding how to avoid student loan debt?

If you're going to take out student loans, think about what you want to do in life. Don't accept rushing to college because you feel like you need to go to college. Think about what the job market is. What's the likelihood of you getting hired directly out of college? Do you need additional experience? How much money are you going to be making? What is the average salary for a starting position? My first job out of college I was making $27,000 a year. When we're looking at those types of things, we need to understand how much we are taking out in student loans. There are certain positions, especially in the medical environment, where you don't have $200,000 to pay for schooling but those positions usually pay substantially more.

Look at potentially starting at a local, two-year college then transferring into a four-year college. I recommend everyone evaluate how long it would take you to pay off any loans.

There are a lot of companies now that are looking at a more wholistic view of hiring employees—not necessarily seeking college degree-level individuals to fill certain positions. Realizing that college is important, but not everyone needs to go to college to be able to get qualified in certain things. For example, there's IT [information technology] certification companies out there for all sorts of different types of technology certifications. You don't need a degree to get them and you don't have to take out student loans to be qualified for them. A lot of companies are looking for those certificated candidates instead of, or on top of, the degrees—depending on the level of position.

7

AMANDA PARHAM

I was raised under the notion that money was not an appropriate topic of conversation.

I met Amanda Parham when she began working with me at HNTB. In fact, at one point she was my boss. One day I overheard a phone conversation she was having in which she mentioned working three jobs in order to pay her way through school. As you would expect, I was intrigued! As soon as she hung up the phone, I mentioned this book project and kindly asked her to consider sharing her story.

At the time of this interview Amanda was 30 years old, single, with no kids. She attended three colleges and in 2013 graduated from Clayton State University in Morrow, Georgia, with a degree in communication/media studies. Although she was unable to avoid student loan debt entirely, she has since paid off all her debt and is living completely debt free. Here's her story:

. . .

What is your view toward money? Did your parents (or anyone else) teach you about money when you were young?

Growing up I knew money was important—it was what enabled my parents to provide for me and themselves. Since both of my parents worked, I realized early on that I would need money to afford the things that I wanted, so I got my first job at 16. Having a job allowed me to do all the extracurricular activities I wanted to do in high school such as going to movies with friends, having meals, and attending concerts and sporting events, but it also taught me responsibility. With the money I made, I paid for gas and insurance for my car. As I got older, I started to pay for more bills.

I would not consider myself financially literate. I did not openly discuss money with my family or friends as I was raised that it was not an appropriate topic of conversation. Today, I am more conscious of spending. I don't have any debt—I've paid off my student loans, credit cards, and most recently I've paid off my car. However, I'm still learning about finances—how to better plan for the future with budgeting, identifying what my financial goals are, and the importance of saving for retirement.

I think it is more of a Southern mentality [to not talk about money]. I've lived in Georgia all my life. I think it was passed on from my grandparents to my parents. You don't want to talk about it [money] because you don't want to boast about financial successes to others but also if you are struggling with finances, you keep that to yourself and don't want others to know. Growing up, my parents probably put more on credit cards then they should, but they wanted to provide for me and make sure I wasn't missing out on anything. From those initial conversations of finances, I didn't understand the full impact of what I know today based on the experiences that I've gone through.

· · ·

Did you graduate college debt free? If so, share your story. How did you do it?

I did not graduate college debt free, but I was pretty close compared to most people. I have friends and family members who graduated with thousands and hundreds of thousands of dollars in student loan debt. I graduated college with around $10,000 in debt. My student debt was attributed to losing the HOPE Scholarship for a few years. The HOPE Scholarship program rewards Georgia students with financial assistance to attend eligible Georgia colleges and universities. Overall, I credit graduating college with minimal debt to using the HOPE Scholarship as a resource, working my way through college, and living at home during college. There were some other hacks I used to cut down on my expenses, but those were the three main things that helped keep my student debt low.

Tell us more about how the HOPE Scholarship works.

The HOPE Scholarship covered full tuition and was eligible to Georgia students who graduated high school and then attended a Georgia public university. At that time, you could attend a private university or college and it would cover partial tuition. You also had to have at least a 3.0 GPA to qualify. Having the HOPE Scholarship covered my tuition at the public college I attended.

I lived at home which cut down on the housing and meal expenses. I also continued to work so I had some income coming in to cover books and additional expenses.

[The reason I lost the HOPE Scholarship] At the time I had the HOPE Scholarship I was also working three different jobs. As you can imagine working that many jobs and attending school full time took its toll. I was working at least 30 hours a week and attending school full time and I did not factor in time to study. Because of this my grades suffered and I lost the

HOPE Scholarship as my GPA no longer met the requirements to obtain it.

Discuss all the jobs you worked while in college to help cut down on student loans.

I always worked in the restaurant industry, so I worked as a waitress and then for a while I was working at a bar as a server and bartender to get those late-night shifts. I also worked in a nursery with children for some additional income.

I initially attended Georgia State University, which is a rather large school, so I was able to find class times that fit around a working schedule. For example, I would attend morning classes on Mondays and Wednesdays, get out and work a lunch shift at one job, then head over to a night shift at my other restaurant job. On the weekends I would do some childcare responsibilities, work at the nursery, then pick up some more restaurant shifts. I always found a way to pick my class schedule that would allow me to work as much as I could —not realizing the amount of time I would need to invest to study and maintain those grades.

What challenges did you face paying your way through schooling?

The biggest challenge was not maintaining good enough grades for financial assistance and not realizing how important that was. I started out at Georgia State and attended two semesters as a commuter student. The end of my second semester is when my GPA dropped below the threshold and I was no longer eligible for the HOPE Scholarship. Georgia State was a more expensive school and I felt like I wasn't performing as well as I thought I would. So to help with bringing down expenses, I transferred schools to a small community college called Gordon State College in Barnesville, Georgia.

At Gordon State I was able to pay for college out of pocket. Tuition wasn't too expensive. I had been working, so I had money to save. Also, I was trying to do everything I could to avoid taking out student loans. While I was paying out of pocket for school, my major did not interest me. So, I only attended there briefly—two semesters.

Then I took a semester off to reevaluate what I wanted to do professionally. During this time, I continued to work and save. I did a lot of research into what I actually wanted to do, what college would be a good fit for me, and how could I get the HOPE Scholarship back. From there I transferred to my third and final school of choice—Clayton State University.

While the tuition at Clayton State was reasonable, it was still slightly more expensive, so that's where I had to take out those student loans to cover the costs because I did not have enough money saved. However, I went into Clayton State knowing that I was determined to get that HOPE Scholarship back to cover tuition for future semesters and to keep that student debt low. I took about $10,000 of student loans out to cover tuition for two-to-three semesters. After a few semesters I was eligible for the HOPE Scholarship again, but I continued to work. I only worked a single job and made time to study so I could maintain those good grades. I found a good balance between school and work.

Were you able to commute from home to all three colleges you attended?

Yes! All three colleges I attended were within an hour radius of where I lived. Starting out at Georgia State, we all know about Atlanta traffic, but typically I could get to college in about 20-30 minutes. Gordon State College was in Barnesville and was my furthest commute—about 45 miles from my house. I tried to schedule my classes to cram them all in two days a week to help with my commute. Clayton State was in my hometown so that was a five-minute commute. That was very convenient.

How were you able to pay off your student loan debt in only two years?

Looking back, I only accumulated about $10,000 of student loan debt. Following graduation, I did not prioritize paying back my student loan debt and waited until it was required to start paying on the loans. I had about a six-month grace period where I was just paying the minimum that was due. I did not realize how high my interest rates were on my student loans and I felt like I wasn't making any progress. While I was continuing to work and take on internships, my income was inconsistent, and I prioritized other things. Within a year and a half, I got my act together. I had my first professional job, had a steady income, and realized the significance of that interest and getting that student loan debt down so that I could live debt free and focus my income elsewhere such as retirement, adult bills, and things like that.

I had a private loan with an interest rate hovering around 15%. After making the minimum payments for my first year out of college I realized, "Hey, this balance isn't going down." I then set a financial goal of paying that off within a year and a half and I did! I also had credit card debt, but I prioritized paying off my student loans first because they had higher interest rates.

After paying off my student loans, credit cards, and car, I'm now completely debt free.

. . .

Looking back, is there anything you would've done differently regarding how you managed money during your college years?

I would've put school first. While working my way through college helped me keep costs low, I ultimately lost my main source of financial assistance because I was stretched too thin by working three jobs at once and my grades suffered. I would encourage any student who has an opportunity for a scholarship to use it as a resource, but remember it can go away in an instant if you don't meet those requirements. Following graduation, I wish that I would have prioritized my student loan debt. I waited until I was forced to start paying on them and I just paid the minimum. I did not do the research to learn what my interest rates would be and set a plan for myself to pay it off. Setting a payment schedule and having an end goal can help anyone who has to take out student loans for assistance.

What are your thoughts on the student loan debt crisis?

The student loan debt crisis blows my mind. The cost of college is substantially outpacing inflation and the cost of living. It's crazy that tuition costs have increased 150% to 200% in the past 10 years. It seems like colleges and universities are too focused on outdoing one another. They are running colleges more like a business by increasing the class sizes, raising tuitions, and building new high-tech facilities instead of focusing on the well-being of current and prospective students. I do value and think that continuing education is important, but you have to have a plan and be willing to see it through.

Share your thoughts on the notion that "Education is 'good debt' because you are investing in yourself." Yet, people are

leaving school (some not even graduating) with debt in the six figures.

I would ask, instead of is it a *good* debt, is it a *reasonable* debt? Continuing education is important, but you have to have a plan for yourself. An individual who is interested in becoming an electrician does not require the same amount of education as someone who is going to become a heart surgeon. The final cost associated to both degrees differ greatly. Not just cost, but also the time they invest into it.

Consider the cost-benefit analysis of the college you are interested in attending, the degree you want to pursue, and weigh the financial costs and benefits to see if you could save more money than you realize. Consider the overall cost of tuition. Are you going to need housing? What types of books and materials are you going to need? What are all the extra fees that the college is going to tack on? Also include the financial aid that you anticipate. What types of scholarship money might someone have versus how much debt are they going to have to take out to cover these costs? Also, think long term. Research your planned major and the profession you want to enter. Will it still be relevant by the time you graduate? My mom was a children's librarian and for the longest time I considered going into library sciences, but she steered me away from that because everything is going digital. People aren't valuing libraries as they would. It's not a specialty anymore.

Calculate any anticipated debt during your college career. How long will it take you to pay off your student loan debt after graduation? Is it worth it? Some professions have student loan forgiveness programs. I have friends who are teachers and doctors and some of their companies and/or school districts they work for may qualify to pay back their student loans. Continue researching what that long-term debt might look like and if there's any opportunities for additional assistance after graduation to help cover those costs.

.   .   .

What advice would you give to students entering college regarding how to avoid student loan debt?

Research and apply for as many scholarships as you can. Any financial assistance can make a difference in the long run. Weigh your options for what school you want to go to. An in-state school is going to be cheaper than an out-of-state school. Consider going to a local college or smaller university for a couple of years to get those core classes under your belt before transferring to your dream school. Evaluate the reason *why* you want to go to a certain college. Are you going for the name, the glory, or the collegiate atmosphere? Or does this school have the best program for you? Also, research the employment rates for recent graduates. You want to make sure the school is helping set you up for success for when you graduate. Prioritize studying and your schoolwork, but if you can have an income during your college career that can help you with those expenses, that's a great opportunity. Any money that you can earn that doesn't require you to take out a loan is a win.

8

DEREK BROTT

Your success has a lot to do with your drive.

I first met Derek Brott when we were coworkers at Kennesaw State University (KSU). While neither of us work there anymore, we've stayed in touch ever since. In fact, Derek designed my website yourmarginmatters.com that I use to post blogs and promote my books. When I told him I was writing a book about how to avoid student loan debt he alerted me of his story. Naturally, I asked him to share it with my readers. Coincidentally, Derek's wife Delena also graduated from KSU debt free.

At the time of our interview Derek was 31 and the father of two boys ages 5 and 2. He is from Dallas, Georgia, and earned a Bachelor's in Business Administration with a concentration in management and marketing from KSU in 2012. Derek now works as an underwriter for a commercial insurance company.

. . .

What is your view toward money? Did your parents (or anyone else) teach you about money when you were young?

My household was split. My mom was very frugal. She grew up that way and probably got that from my grandfather—who still is very frugal. When she was in high school, she saved money to buy her first car. She is not afraid to go to garage sales and buy discounted stuff. While my dad does have some frugal tendencies, he never let money stop him from taking care of us or blocking his happiness. If he wanted to do something, take us out to dinner, or go on a trip, we were doing it. There was a lot of contrast in the house. Growing up I didn't really understand that a lot of people fight about money. Now as an adult I can understand and admire both sides.

My mom took me to a Dave Ramsey Financial Peace class while I was in high school. That was my first exposure to money management. She always taught us the value of saving and the value of money. At the time I didn't really grasp it, but it made me a lot better because I was exposed to it early. I've since attended and led several different Dave Ramsey classes.

How did you graduate college debt free?

I went to Kennesaw State University (KSU) and earned a degree in business and marketing. I graduated debt free by using many different avenues. I don't know that I'm a typical story. There are at least five different ways I went about graduating debt free. First, I spent my first year and a half at a technical college [Chattahoochee Technical College]. The tuition was half to a third of what it typically is at a four-year university, so I got my core classes taken care of and I made sure all the credits would transfer.

The second way I went about earning a debt-free degree was qualifying for the HOPE Scholarship. I had made decent enough grades in high school and in my first few semesters at technical college to earn the scholarship, which is funded by the lottery here in Georgia. That was a big help the first couple of semesters as it covered a third to two thirds of the tuition cost. This was especially helpful when I transferred to KSU and the tuition jumped dramatically. Then I also qualified for a few smaller scholarships later on in college.

Third, my grandparents set aside some money for me to go to college. That was a big help for me the first couple of years. They didn't have a big fund to pay for everything, but it was certainly enough to help out.

Fourth, once I transferred to KSU I took a job on campus. The on-campus job was a huge benefit because it helped me stay focused on my studies as the job provided the flexibility to allow me to take time off to study as needed. This also gave me a peek behind the curtain as I got to know advisors and financial aid staffers. Therefore, I was in the know regarding how to get through college debt free by using the different avenues and resources the university provides. Also by making a paycheck I was able to pay for my books every semester. Additionally, as a university employee, I was granted access to the bookstore early so I could obtain the cheaper, used versions of the books I needed. After I graduated, I was hired by the university as a full-time employee and had the opportunity to continue my education with tuition assistance programs (TAP).

Lastly, my dad always made sure we were taken care of. Any time I came up short he was always there to help make up the difference.

Did you live on campus or at home?

I lived at home my first year, then I lived on campus for a semester or two at KSU, but once I realized how much it was and seeing what it was doing to my bank account, I knew that lifestyle not sustainable. However, it was convenient. There were times I didn't drive my truck for over a week while living on campus. I'd walk to class and walk to work. It was a big help, but it was a pretty penny.

After that I moved off campus to an apartment for a little while. During my senior year I lived in another house that was very cheap.

What challenges did you face paying your way through schooling?

I lost the HOPE Scholarship as a result of withdrawing from a class. Unfortunately, I made an error in the timing of my withdrawal and the class was counted as a fail. This caused me to lose my HOPE. That was rough. I fell below the GPA threshold to maintain the HOPE Scholarship and worked my butt off to regain it over the next two semesters. That was a big struggle. There was a lot of scraping and clawing.

My dad didn't go to college, but he was very adamant that his kids go to college and that they graduate debt free. We were always brainstorming on how we could make it work—searching for scholarships we could apply for. I found it awkward asking my parents and grandparents for money. There was always that weird time right before the semester started when I had to ask, "So...can I have some money?" However, I took a lot of pride in contributing as I worked a lot of hours. It was having that grit and determination of "I'm going to get this done no matter what it takes."

What other scholarships did you apply for?

While I can't remember the names, they were some of the

smaller ones—$500, etc. My wife also graduated debt free and I always remember her story because she got on with the Pell Grant. My biggest advice regarding scholarships is go talk to the advisors. Talk to the people who spend every day looking at scholarship applications. A lot of the applications are essay based and the advisors can give you tips on how to write the essays properly. They don't expect perfect essays. They are looking for the quality of the content you write.

Looking back, is there anything you would've done differently regarding how you managed money during your college years?

I wish I would've spent more time with my advisors—scholarship and academic advisors. Having a professional to steer you makes all the difference in the world. There is so much information out there that it is easy to drown in it. Having somebody to help you sort through all the resources is so beneficial. I definitely wish I would've spent more time doing that. Of course, I wish I would've saved more money that I earned from my on-campus jobs. Taco Bell and Krystal got more of my paycheck than they should have.

When I graduated college, it took me about a year to find a decent, full-time employer. It was a weird time in the economy. Thank God that I graduated debt free! Having that [student loan debt] over your head over a year after you graduate is not ideal. Remember universities have great marketing teams and your parents will tell you, "You have to go to college. You're going to get a great job. You're going to make a ton of money. If you go in there and get your four-year degree, you'll spend a ton of money to make a ton of money." No. That's not true. There are plenty of people who have done that, but that's not the rule.

Besides focusing on school, I wish I would've been more focused on building up a decent savings.

What are your thoughts on the student loan debt crisis?

It sucks. I don't know how else to explain it. I couldn't image being an 18, 19, or 20 year old and having that kind of debt hanging over your head every day. I get it. I understand 100% why they want it forgiven. Those [student] loan programs have great marketing teams. They are in your face and they sell the green pastures. They make it seem like this is the only way to do it and it's the best way to do it. When you're that young you don't know. You assume that everyone has your best interest at heart. It does bother me. Being on the other side of it and knowing how adamant my dad was about graduating debt free, I make sure every college kid I come in contact with knows what a difference it will make to graduate without debt. It will change your world.

You got into college and racked up $100,000 of debt and you come out making a $40,000 a year. You're trying to live. You don't have the bandwidth to pay those loans off. That's something that follows you and it's why everyone gets so excited when they pay them off. It's freeing.

I'm drawn to the work that Mike Rowe from the TV show "Dirty Jobs" does. He's very open and honest to the fact that there are so many other opportunities compared to a four-year degree. A lot of the guys that I graduated high school with— several of them went to college but several didn't go to college. Several went into the trades; several got technical degrees and went into the IT industry. By the time I graduated from a four-year university these guys had gone and got a two-year degree and jumped into the field making a ton of money. So, if money is your end goal, a four-year degree isn't always the best answer.

Some of the guys that went to a trade went into a five-year apprentice program. Their school was paid for as part of the program, they had full benefits, and were getting paid $15 to $20 an hour right out of high school. Going to a four-year university and taking out $100,000 of student loans isn't always the answer.

What is the root cause of the student loan debt crisis?

The first thing that comes to mind is profit. These [loan] companies know how to take advantage of very young, impressionable minds. All these credit card companies do the same thing. Discover Card spends so much money to market to and secure 18 year olds to become card holders because they know their customer base will stay around for a long time. I was one of the victims. I think that's the root cause.

I get that someone may not have all the resources to obtain a degree but there are so many scholarships out there. Many companies will now help you pay for college. There are so many opportunities where you can make money and get help versus getting this huge loan that you pay interest on for the next 25 years.

Share your thoughts on the notion that "Education is 'good debt' because you are investing in yourself." Yet, people are leaving school (some not even graduating) with debt in the six figures.

First and foremost, make sure college is for you. I'm referring to a traditional four-year university where you are going to amass $100,000+ of debt. That's where you are going to be marketed to in order to get the most amount of money out of you. I know that job applications ask you where you went to college and what your degree was in, but at the end of the day it doesn't really matter—except for maybe the top 1% of jobs in individual industries. I know a lot of guys who are very intelligent engineers that went to a technical school. They didn't go to a four-year university in order to obtain a big engineering degree. Your success has a lot to do with your drive.

There are so many opportunities out there which allow a person to get hands-on experience, while getting an education, with it being paid for. It's not a bad route to go. Everybody thought the end-all, be-all answer was, you go to a big fancy school, you get a big fancy degree, and then you get a big fancy job. That's the exception, not the rule. Some of the wealthiest people in the world never went to college.

I'm not bashing college. I have a four-year degree at the second-largest university in Georgia. It was a great opportunity for me. It shook out a lot of my adolescence. I always had an interest in marketing and the classes and professors there were amazing. I thoroughly enjoyed getting my degree. Really think about what you want to do and if you're not sure maybe you start out at a technical college to knock out your core classes. Then you will still have the opportunity to transfer to a larger university, but you do it at half the price.

What advice would you give to students entering college regarding how to avoid student loan debt?

As a middle school or high school student, try to get out and be exposed to different industries and job opportunities. I think it will give you a lot of clarity on what direction you might go. I wouldn't focus on what you want to do, I would focus on what you do *not* want to do. What does not seem interesting? What doesn't look like fun? That will narrow you down and determine your direction. Some people love being outside. Some people love freedom and don't want a desk job. Others enjoy technical skills. By creating some clarity in which direction you might want to go, ultimately that's how you can avoid the debt. If you're interested in a field, it will make you want that degree even more and will push you to work harder in order to achieve better grades. In turn you'll have more scholarship opportunities and you'll make more money.

PART III

THE SOLUTIONS

9

WAYS TO PAY FOR COLLEGE

An ounce of prevention is worth a pound of cure. – Benjamin Franklin

---

Paying for college is a challenge for most families and often involves tapping into a variety of sources. Asking "How do I pay for college?" is like asking, "How do I get healthy?" There are numerous answers, but there's not always one clear path. If you're like most students and families, you'll pool together funds from multiple resources. As Benjamin Franklin famously said, "An ounce of prevention is worth a pound of cure,"—especially when it comes to student loan debt. In other words, you're a lot better off devising a plan now in order to avoid potential student loans in the future. How do you avoid loans when you're short on rich family members, trust fund cash, and a winning lottery ticket? Here are some strategies to consider:

.   .   .

Work

This should be the glaringly obvious choice. While some students might say, "I don't want to work because I want to focus on my studies," unfortunately that is not the reality for most. A part-time, 20-hour-a-week job can help pay for college-related expenses. Whether you work on or off campus, having that income can help you pay for your education and help reduce or even eliminate what amount you may need to borrow.

As a matter of convenience, explore what on-campus jobs are available. Many students work part time in the university cafeteria to pay for some of their living expenses. Plus, after the shift, you might get a free meal, which could save you about $50 a week. Most on-campus jobs are easy and flexible—allowing you to work around your class schedule. Some campus jobs also offer tuition waivers and pay you a one-time stipend check. This is more common at the graduate level with graduate assistant (GA) positions. For example, a GA could work as an assistant in his/her program's department. By working part time, 20-hours a week, the student would receive full-tuition waiver along with a $2,000-$5,000 stipend check at the end of the semester.

If you want to avoid working while school's in session, look for jobs over the summer or winter holidays to earn money to put toward the coming semester. Start a side hustle if you want more flexibility in your work schedule but still want to earn money to help pay for college.

Additionally, you could potentially work a full-time job during the day and attend classes at night. That's how I got through grad school. Most universities are now offering online, hybrid, or directed studies that don't require students to physically attend class. There are so many options now that allow students to create a flexible class schedule which then provides windows of time to earn an income.

Finally, there is no shame in taking a gap year and working in order to save money for school. I'd rather work my butt off for a year than have to pay off student loans for 20.

Employer Tuition Reimbursement

Instead of paying for your education on your own, work for an employer that offers assistance. Several companies, such as Chipotle, Disney, Starbucks, Home Depot, UPS, AT&T, Verizon, Best Buy, Publix, Amazon, and Wells Fargo, are willing to help you pay for your education. As previously mentioned, my current employer HNTB's tuition reimbursement program paid for my final semester of grad school. It saved me about $3,000. Some companies may offer a program that isn't advertised. Check with your human resources department to find out. Although you likely won't have the entire cost covered, any help is worth having.

Apply for Scholarships and Grants

There are about $100 million in unclaimed scholarships each year simply because students don't know they exist.

There is a tremendous amount of money out there that goes unused every year that could help pay for your college expenses. I'm convinced the reason is one of two things: 1) people don't know the money is available; 2) people are intimidated by the application process—meaning they think there will be too much competition for the money.

While it can seem hopeless to apply for a bunch of college scholarships that require hours of preparation with little chance of getting anything in the end, going after free money for college can absolutely help you avoid loans and debt, even if some work is involved upfront. Since scholarships seem to be a dime a dozen these days, it helps to have a specific plan before you dive in. Perhaps the best way to unearth scholarships and grants involves looking local. These are the lowest hanging fruit because they naturally have less competition. To find local scholarships you may not have to fight for, look for local community foundations, credit unions, doctor offices, law offices, Elks Clubs, Rotary Clubs, and any other local businesses that may offer funding. You can also check with your school's guidance office since local businesses and organizations often email their applications to local high schools and colleges to keep on hand.

No scholarship is too small. Even if you get $2,500 from your local credit union or $1,000 from the Rotary Club, that's money you don't have to worry about later. Don't forget to apply for scholarships at your choice schools. You could end up with a four-year, full-tuition offer. Keep applying for scholarships even while you're in college. You can get funding to help cover books, housing, and other costs even as a sophomore or junior.

An online scholarship search tool like some of the following can help you find scholarships to pay for college.

- **Scholarships.com** has a database of scholarships worth more than $19 billion. Once you sign up and create a profile, you can filter and browse through the scholarships available.

- **Fastweb** has scholarships worth more than $3.4 billion. Students just need to sign up to browse for available scholarships and grants.

- **Chegg** offers a number of scholarships, including thousands that don't require you to write an essay. If you choose not to sign up, you can still browse according to your location and type of application.

More scholarship websites can be found in the Resources section in the back of this book.

Chick-fil-A Remarkable Futures Scholarship

As a staff member of Chick-fil-A in the mid-90s, I was fortunate to receive its $1,000 scholarship award. At the time the benchmarks for acceptance included working with the company for two years and logging 2,000 hours on the job. As much as that money helped me then, Chick-fil-A has since greatly enhanced its scholarship program opportunities. According to its website, Chick-fil-A now awards two types of scholarships to employees—True Inspiration Scholarships ($25,000/each) and Leadership Scholarships ($2,500/each). These scholarships are awarded annually, which means if you stay employed with the company during your college career you can potentially win multiple scholarships.

In 2020, Chick-fil-A awarded $17 million in scholarships to 6,700 of its team members. The scholarship money can be used at any accredited two- or four-year college, university, or technical/vocational school. In addition to scholarships, Chick-fil-A has a network of more than 100 colleges and universities offering discounts to its employees. The list includes private institutions such as Boston University and Oglethorpe University, public research institutions like Purdue University, and many online universities and programs.

Many employers offer scholarship programs. Do your research to discovery the best opportunities.

. . .

Dual Enrollment

This one is huge for cutting college expenses. Some states allow students to earn college credit for classes taken during high school. These classes are usually taught to a higher standard and credit is issued through a public university. Depending on where you live, the credits earned in this manner can be transferred to state schools. If you happen to have a college near you that offers dual enrollment, you could save a ton of money on school tuition. Dual enrollment courses are often offered completely free or at steep discounts compared to the tuition fees of most colleges.

The first time I was exposed to the dual enrollment program was during my time as a grad student at Kennesaw State. There I was a 42-year-old grown man sitting next to a 17-year-old high school student. [That class was cross listed—meaning it had undergraduate and graduate students in the same class.] As you might imagine, I struck up a conversation with the young lad as he proceeded to blow my mind on the dual enrollment program opportunity. My mind was spinning with ideas of how to get my then 2-year-old son signed up for the program.

Here's how it works in my home state of Georgia:

Georgia has created a singular program known as Dual Enrollment for students in grades 9-12 who qualify to participate. Students may enroll on a part-time or full-time basis as a Dual Enrollment student and take college courses at their high school or on a postsecondary campus. Students will receive high school and college credit simultaneously when attending and passing approved college classes.

Dual Enrollment, which allows students to take college courses and earn college credits while still in high school, is one of the state's most popular education initiatives. Since its beginning almost three decades ago, it has been touted as a way to give high school students an early start on college while saving their parents money.

Basically, my classmate explained that by dual enrolling he was able to knock out his first year of college classes—at the expense of the state—and start college as a sophomore. A savings of time and money. Each state's offering may differ. If your state offers a similar program it could save you thousands!

Take AP Classes in High School

Taking Advanced Placement (AP) classes in high school can help you earn college credit alongside your diploma and lead to tuition savings as an undergraduate. AP classes prepare individuals to take tests on college-level knowledge in 38 subjects, including English, social science, math, and various languages. Students who receive passing scores on these tests can earn college credit, saving time and money.

Rather than paying college tuition prices for a class, learners pay one exam fee. As a result, AP credits allow students to skip introductory classes once they start college. Additionally, these courses help high schoolers gain admission to competitive colleges. An AP class shows colleges that an applicant can complete college-level work.

Please note: Not every school offers AP classes. Check with your local school(s) or school district(s).

Student Research Positions

To help cover college expenses, students might also be able

to work on certain projects as undergraduate researchers. Not only do these types of roles help pay some of the bills, but they also provide real-world experience that can help students land jobs after graduation.

Look for positions in an area in which you have experience. Also check with your professors and other teachers for anyone looking for undergraduate assistants. Organizations outside of your school, such as hospitals, research institutions, and community-based organizations often look for students to fill research positions that are backed by grants.

Internships

Like research positions, internships can be a way to build some real-world experience while in school. Most internships offer you some type of course credit and some come with the added bonus of being paid. However, paid internships can be difficult to land, depending on your field. Visit your school's career center for information about available paid opportunities. Don't discount the possibility of finding a paid internship by networking with family and friends.

Work-Study Programs

You can also look into work-study programs that can help supply you with an income while you attend undergraduate or graduate courses, although federal work-study programs are mostly offered to students who can exhibit financial need.

To qualify for federal work-study programs, you must be in pursuit of a postsecondary educational degree or certificate. The hourly wages you'll be paid are legally required to be higher than the federal minimum wage, and jobs that are compatible with work-study can include your school itself, a federal, state, or local public agency, any private nonprofit organization, or a private, for-profit organization.

Like other federal programs, determining eligibility for a federal work-study program starts with filling out a Free Application for Federal Student Aid, or FAFSA form.

Final Thoughts

As you can see there are many ways to pay for college. Unfortunately, when it comes to higher education, our culture tells us to borrow a ton of money then spend decades paying it off. Don't let anyone tell you that you have to take out expensive loans to pay for college. There are plenty of other options to consider (in addition to what I've provided), and they can all lead to the type of career you are passionate about and an income you desire.

I hope that the aforementioned suggestions have sparked some ideas that will create a new path allowing you to obtain the educational experience you want without spending a lifetime in debt. Odds are, with the soaring cost of college, you'll require more than one tactic to pay for school. There's a lot of grant and scholarship money out there unknown to most people. Carefully research the cost of attendance at the school of your choice and devise a plan that allows you to meet those costs as efficiently as possible. Dare I say—create a budget.

10

WAYS TO SAVE WHILE IN COLLEGE

It always seems impossible until it's done. - Nelson Mandela

I reflect fondly on the saying, "Live like a college student." This doesn't have to mean eating ramen noodles and rolling pennies to save money. It simply means being creative, resourceful, and wise with your lifestyle choices. Keep in mind that the key to financial success is being aware of how you're spending your money. Once again, this is where creating a simple budget can prove beneficial.

The idea of saving money in college might sound absurd— but it's totally achievable. The more money you can save during college, the more prepared and confident you'll be entering the real world after graduation. You might be surprised to discover all the ways you can save money during your collegiate career. Here's a list of my favorites that should help reduce some of college's biggest expenses.

. . .

Attend an In-State School

The average tuition at a public, in-state school is $10,230 per year, and the average tuition at a public, out-of-state school is $26,290 per year. That's an annual difference of more than $16,000 and a four-year difference of a whopping $64,000. Out-of-state, private college rates are even higher.

Live at Home

For those who are fortunate enough to have this option, it's well worth taking advantage of. I understand the feeling of wanting to get away from your family but living at home is one of the best ways to save money in college—assuming you are attending school near your home. Even if your parents charge you a nominal rent, that's probably going to save you so much more than trying to live on or off campus. Although you'll have some commuting expenses, you should still experience significant cost savings. Living at home while in school can dramatically change your financial position after graduation.

Work

Are you detecting a theme here? Working is essential for every college student. Not only does it give you a little money, but it also teaches you invaluable life skills such as budgeting, problem solving, time management, and planning. Why is working in college on a list of ways to *save money* while in college you might ask? Because if you're working, you're not out spending money—you're earning and hopefully saving it.

Living On or Off Campus

Renting an apartment isn't always going to be cheaper than living on campus, and campus housing isn't always going to be cheaper than renting. Research all the options available at your school and the nearby college town to see what's most afford- able. Don't forget to factor in utilities and transportation costs. You can also save money by having roommates to split the bills.

Becoming a Resident Advisor

Become a resident assistant. College dorms usually employ a resident assistant (usually an upperclassman) to help younger students and keep the peace. You will have to live in the dorm, but the rooms are almost always private. These rooms are often free or heavily discounted and sometimes resident assistants are even given a monthly stipend.

Ditch Your Car

Most college students don't need a car mainly because they live on or near campus. Do you know how much it costs for the privilege of owning an automobile? According to AAA, the average annual cost of car ownership is about $9,000 a year. That's a substantial savings of $36,000 if you're one of the lucky ones to get your degree in four years. If you're like me and it takes six years to obtain your bachelor's, that's $54,000 back in your pocket.

Today's society offers a plethora of ways to commute. On campus, you can walk, bike, skateboard, scooter, or bum rides. Additionally, many college campuses have free buses and shut- tles that help students get around campus and even to nearby apartments and shopping centers. Kennesaw State, for exam- ple, has the B.O.B. (Big Owl Bus) that shuttles students between campuses along with local retail outlets. Some apartment complexes have shuttles for students to get to campus. Depending on your school, see if you can leverage free trans- portation to get around.

To travel off campus, you can always use public transit (if available in your area), borrow a friend's car, or use a Zipcar if you need to travel long distance. Rideshare services such as Uber and Lyft are also affordable ways to get around when you need to venture off campus.

Never Buy New Textbooks

The price of new textbooks can cause your blood pressure to spike with some costing in the $200 range. I remember nearly fainting after reading the syllabus of my Technical Writing class that required me to acquire seven books. Before you blow the budget at the campus bookstore, see if you can borrow books from a fellow student or from the university library. If not, buy or rent used textbooks from Amazon. You can also rent books from Chegg, Barnes & Noble's textbook service, or order digital textbooks through sites like iFlipd, which offer a pay-as-you-go model. Being resourceful with your textbook usage can lead to tons of savings.

Maximize Campus Amenities

You might be surprised at all the amenities your tuition fees cover. Take advantage of what your campus has to offer in terms of activities instead of spending money on going out. Many campuses have an array of museums, offer movie nights and other social events for cheaper or, sometimes, for free (meaning you've already paid for them through your student activities fees as part of your tuition). You certainly don't need to pay $50 a month for a gym membership if your college has a workout facility you can use.

Perhaps one of the most underappreciated and overlooked building is the library. In addition to books, college libraries usually have computers, videos, software, and more. This is all available to students at no additional cost. The library can become your best friend if you're progressing through college on a budget. Additionally, several college athletic events will offer complimentary game tickets to students. Research what your school's activity and athletic fees cover and you might be surprised at all that's available to you.

Cut Cable

Do you really need to pay $100 a month for 300 channels you'll never watch? Cutting your cable could easily save you $1,200 a year, or more. Explore cheaper alternatives like Netflix (basic plan $8.99/month), Hulu (starting at $5.99/month), and a HDTV antenna (provides local channels for free). My wife and I bought a smart TV and a HDTV antenna. Expecting to get the four local broadcast channels (ABC, NBC, CBS, FOX) I was pleasantly surprised to see around 60-70 over-the-air channels that were available to watch for free and in fabulous HD! Also, I was astonished with options as to how much embedded streaming content comes inside a smart TV. Did I mention the cost of TVs has dramatically dropped? We bought a 51-inch smart VIZIO TV for $299 at Target. Has your time arrived to cut the cord?

Ask for Student Discounts

Don't leave home without your student ID. So many places offer student discounts, but so few people ask for them. These include restaurants, shops, movie theaters, theme parks, and more. Discounts are available on everything from clothing to laptop and notebook computers (see next section) for those with a valid student ID. For example, Apple, and Adobe offer reduced prices on tech, while hundreds of big brands give money off on clothing. Most of the restaurants surrounding my school offer student deals ranging from 10% to 25% off your food bill. Before you pay full price, see if there's a student discount. This is a simple way to save some extra money in college for just going to school.

Discounts on Computer Hardware and Software

Another big expense for college is technology. Many students want (or need) to get a new laptop, and with that comes all the additional cost of software. Plus, some classes require their own specific software that you need to install. If you're getting any type of new computer or software, make sure you purchase it through the education store to secure your education discount. Most companies offer significant discounts to students—from Apple and Microsoft, to Adobe and more. No matter what technology you need, you can probably secure a big discount by buying an "education edition." Upon starting grad school, I saved over $100 on a new laptop from Best Buy simply by showing them my student email address. In fact, if you submit your student email on Best Buy's website, they will email you exclusive coupons for student discounts.

Learn to Cook

Do your best to limit eating meals out. If you bought your school's meal plan, use it. Student discounts aside, the costs of eating out can add up quickly. Consider investing in a good coffee maker instead of spending money every morning on lattes. It's almost always cheaper to cook than it is to go out and buy premade food. While a dinner for $7 to $10 may sound cheap, it adds up over time. You can probably cook the same meal (and prep for future meals) for about half the price. Cooking isn't difficult, but it does take some practice and patience. Getting started with easy meals like crockpot recipes can really be a confidence boost. Then you can have potlucks with your roommates and friends to share food.

Attend Events with Free Food

How do you get starving college students to attend an event? You guessed it, free food! There are so many events that take place on college campuses, and many include food. I can't even count how many free pizza events I went to when I was in college. The strategy is to look for signs, posters, and promotions around your campus. Additionally, events will be announced on the school's website, social media channels, and through student email listservs. These announcements usually promote free food in an attempt to lure students to come. I know you may feel like a scavenger by doing this, but if you think about the enormous cost of food, the amount of money you'll be saving, plus the fact that you've probably already paid for this through your tuition and activity fees, it's a no-brainer. I was so frugal, I had this down to a science. If you do this regularly, you can probably get your lunch taken care of most days and maybe you'll even learn something and make new friends at the events.

Family Cell Phone Plan

Check with your provide to see if you can get on a family cell phone plan with your parents. Most wireless carriers offer an option to add a line to an existing plan. If you aren't already, jumping onto your parents' family plan is much less expensive than opening your own. Simply pay your parents the monthly difference (usually between $15 and $50). When I was on a single-line plan I paid around $85 a month. Since joining a family plan I pay $30 a month.

. . .

Earn Your Degree in Four Years

One of the best ways to save money in college is to simply have a solid plan for your classes and degree program. Earning a bachelor's degree in four years, as opposed to five or six, can save you thousands. Contrary to popular belief, college is not the time to *find yourself*—it's too expensive. You should be going to college with a specific purpose. Ensuring that you're taking the right classes and progressing to earn your degree on time is a great way to save money in college. Every extra class and semester costs money. Better yet, if you can earn college credit while still in high school (see previous chapter), do it! By knocking out several classes or credits early, you might even be able to graduate early and save money.

Final Thoughts

The list above provides just some of the many ways you can save money while in college in an effort to avoid graduating with a debt sentence. College is the perfect training ground to allow you to learn the skills of minimalism, frugality, and resourcefulness. You may feel like you are sacrificing a great deal, but you are also preparing yourself for life.

Experiences are more important than things. And experiences (especially in college) can be free or very cheap. You don't need to spend more money than you have to impress people. What's more impressive is saving money while in college, investing it, and becoming financially independent in your early 30s. That's a great goal right there.

11

ALTERNATIVES TO TRADITIONAL COLLEGE

Formal education will make you a living; self-education will make you a fortune. – Jim Rohn

---

What do Steve Jobs, Bill Gates, Mark Zuckerberg, Michael Dell, Larry Ellison, Ted Turner, Dave Thomas, and Paul Allen have in common? They represent some of the wealthiest and most influential entrepreneurs in the world. None of them have a college degree. College isn't for everyone and that's OK. If I hadn't been accepted into Kennesaw State, there was no higher education plan B. I would've just gone to work. Today the alternatives to either starting at or forgoing a traditional college are plentiful. Let's explore some different options:

ATTEND COMMUNITY COLLEGE FIRST

According to recent statistics from College Board, one year at a public, four-year, in-state institution cost students an average of

$10,440 in tuition and fees for the 2019-2020 school year, while one year in a two-year, community college was just $3,730—a savings of $6,710 per year!

As you can see, it makes a ton of sense to attend community college for a few years before transferring to a four-year school. With this strategy, you can complete your general course requirements at a community college where tuition is much lower, and you could potentially live at home and save even more. With tuition so low, working your way through school and paying as you go with part-time work also becomes infinitely easier.

Besides potentially saving tens of thousands of dollars, there are many other benefits to starting at a two-year school. Here are a few things to consider:

- **Smaller Classes** – Because of the smaller class sizes, professors are more likely to know you by name and be more available for one-on-one help. Many students learn better with more individualized attention, especially right after high school. Transitioning from a classroom with 20-30 peers to a lecture hall with more than 100 other students can be overwhelming, intimidating, and can make learning challenging.

- **Flexibility** – Community colleges are used to accommodating the busy schedules of full-time workers and parents. If you have a family or job that you have to balance while taking classes, you'll find more flexibility at a community college than you will at a state university. Between night classes and online courses, you can customize a schedule that works for you.

- **Transfer Your Credits** – No matter where you decide to begin your education, you can always graduate elsewhere. Most states have a transfer program set up so that you can attend a community college for your first two years and finish your degree at a bigger school. If you do plan on finishing your education at a different school, make sure the credits you earn will transfer. Check with the university you plan on transferring to and stay in contact with counselors as well as academic advisors to ensure you're taking the right classes.

- **Job Opportunities** – Continuing your education in any capacity will pave the way for more job opportunities. If you don't have a college degree in the field you're pursuing, attending a community college will help to open more doors for you in the job market. In fact, there are several high-paying jobs that don't require a four-year college degree (see list later in this chapter).

Final Thoughts

Several friends have told me that if they would've just started at a two-year school first then went on to the traditional college of their choice, they could have avoided at least half of their student loan debt. Research what community college options are available in your area and determine the potential cost savings you might be able to take advantage of.

An associate degree requires half the time, much less than half the money, and opens doors to some high-quality, in-demand jobs including:

- Radiation therapist
- Dental hygienist
- Registered nurse
- Air traffic controller
- Computer programmer
- Paralegal
- Police officer
- Aerospace engineer

A recent Ramsey Solutions study interviewed over 10,000 millionaires and found that 79% did not attend prestigious private colleges or universities. Almost 80% of Americans built their wealth without a pricey degree.

ONLINE COLLEGE

The perks of taking online classes (also known as distance learning) are numerous. Did you know you can earn a certificate, or associate, bachelor's, or master's degree online? These courses offer additional flexibility for busy students, especially for those balancing school with work and family. They can attract professionals looking for career advancement, parents seeking to better provide for their families, and returning students looking to pick up where they left off. Some online programs even provide additional control over the pace of learning.

Several years ago, Starbucks made the news when they announced a free tuition program for its employees if they attended online college. According to its website: "Every benefits-eligible U.S. partner working part- or full-time receives 100% tuition coverage for a first-time bachelor's degree through Arizona State University's online program. Choose from over

100 diverse undergraduate degree programs and have our support every step of the way." Employees must work for Starbucks for at least three months and at least 20 hours per week to take advantage of these benefits. Many other employers have similar job benefits and perks. Research what companies may offer before you consider applying.

Some schools offer only online classes, while many brick-and-mortar colleges host online courses in addition to in-person ones. Depending on your school's offerings, and your location and preference, you can take all your classes online, or take some online and some in-person. Either way, research the school carefully before enrolling to make sure it's affordable, properly accredited, and has a track record of preparing students for success after graduation.

The Advantages of Online College

- **Cost** – It's no secret that college costs a lot of money. You pay for classes, a dorm room, cafeteria meals, activity fees, textbooks, and other incidentals. It adds up quick. There's a reason most students have to take out loans. With online classes, you're only paying for the university credits. If you're trying to save money, this is a perfect solution.

- **Convenience** – You can attend class at home, in an airport, or out-of-town, as long as you have a reliable internet connection.

- **Access** – You may live or work in an area where the program you need or prefer is not offered by the traditional institutions. Online access can open a world of options.

- **Flexibility** – Online courses offer flexibility not often found in traditional programs. Having access to course materials online, 24/7, means that you can schedule the majority of your study and course review time around your other commitments, such as work and family.

Final Thoughts

Taking online classes may be a departure from the traditional classroom, but for many it's a change for the better. This option brings the experience straight to you, allowing you to work at your own pace to make a better life for you and your family. Best of all, taking online classes allows you to integrate your studies into your schedule at your convenience. Online learning isn't for everyone and you have to be self-motivated and disciplined enough to keep up with the work. However, It can be a good option for parents, full-time workers, and students with disabilities.

TECHNICAL/TRADE SCHOOL

A trade school, also known as a technical or vocational school, is an educational institution that exists to teach skills related to a specific job. Due to the increasingly high costs associated with a college education, more people have been considering trade school as an education alternative.

Trade schools are a more streamlined approach to education, with curricula focusing on developing a particular skill set and knowledge base for a career rather than receiving a general education. Trade schools typically take a lot less time to complete, have smaller class sizes, and the majority of the training is hands-on, which is an ideal environment for many types of learners. Vocational degrees can lead to well-paying jobs like electrician, mechanic, machinist, pharmacy technician, nuclear technician, and dental hygienist, with room for growth and managerial potential in each field.

Advantages to Trade Schools

- **Salaries** – For starters, salaries for trade school graduates aren't that much of a drop off compared to a four-year degree. According to the National Center for Educational Statistics, technical and trade school jobs have a median annual salary of $35,720, though this figure varies heavily based on the industry, demand of position, geographic region, and the experience level of the worker. The Bureau of Labor Statistics (BLS) predicted earnings for bachelor's degree holders to be roughly $46,900, amounting to an annual difference of $11,180. This stat, of course, doesn't factor in long-term earnings growth. However, because trade school only takes an average of two years to complete versus four, that amounts to an additional two years of income for the trade school graduate, or $71,440. Factor in another $70,000 in costs for the many students who take an extra year to graduate from college, and trade school grads can be over $140,000 ahead from the get-go, making up for over 12 years of difference in income.

- **Cost of Education** – The average trade school degree costs $33,000, which, compared to a $127,000 bachelor's degree, means a savings of $94,000. Additionally, if you assume that students are fully financing their education with loans at 4% over 10 years, the bachelor's degree will cost $154,000, while the trade school degree will cost only $40,000. That's a savings of $114,000 just on the degree. Of course, most students in both cases won't fully finance their education. They'll work and find other sources of income to help with the process, meaning the gap will be smaller in the average case. The average college student debt load is $29,900, and that number rises to $36,327 when factoring in interest. Conversely, the average debt load for students graduating from a two-year technical school is $10,000, roughly 70% less than the four-year graduate.

- **Job Security** – Yet another advantage of technical trade school is that most of the jobs you'll qualify for are extremely difficult to export to another country. More and more jobs are being outsourced to places where labor is cheaper, making domestic employment in certain sectors difficult to obtain. It is much easier to export computer programming work, or other information economy work, than it is to export carpentry or electrical work, as that requires a physical presence. Not only that, but there's a growing domestic demand for high-precision talent and skills. According to Forbes, skilled trade workers are a disproportionately older population, and will only continue to get older and eventually retire, creating increased opportunities for young workers to fill their shoes.

* * *

DON'T BE LIKE JON. MAKE SURE THERE'S DEMAND IN YOUR FIELD.

JON
- 4-year degree in a field with no jobs
- Over $100K in debt
- Thinks people who don't go to college are stupid
- Can't find work

RON
- 4-year paid apprenticeship
- Completely debt free
- Earns over $80K a year
- Cut Jon's power for nonpayment

A meme designed to promote the benefits of trade/technical school.

Career Paths

The following represent some of the careers you can pursue with a technical college degree, along with their average yearly salaries, according to the BLS. Please note that the salaries will vary on a variety of factors including experience, demand, and geographic region, etc.

- Construction management: $91,370
- Network Systems Administrator: $81,100
- Dental hygienist: $74,070
- Sonographer: $73,200
- Registered nurse: $70,000

- Web developer: $67,990
- Line installer and repairer for power companies: $64,190
- Police officer: $62,960
- Aircraft mechanic: $61,260
- Respiratory therapist: $59,710
- Cardiovascular technologist: $55,270
- Commercial diver: $55,270
- Electrician: $54,110
- Plumber: $52,590
- Paralegal: $50,410
- HVAC technician: $47,080
- Surgical technologist: $46,310
- Welder: $40,240
- Massage therapist: $39,990
- Automotive technician: $39,550
- EMT or Paramedic: $33,380 (EMT earnings can vary)

* * *

Real-Life Story: Dennis Melendez

My brother-in-law, Dennis Melendez, is an example of an individual who has enjoyed a successful career by learning job-specific skills at a technical training school. Dennis attended Miami's Coral Gables High School and was part of the school's magnet program. He received a two-year academic scholarship to attend Miami Dade Community College. The school now offers four-year degree programs and has been renamed Miami Dade College (MDC).

After attending MDC for a few semesters Dennis received a D in one of his courses. As a result, he lost his scholarship and was forced to find other means to pay for his schooling. Having to work, save, and pay for his education became a challenge. Dennis could not earn enough money to continue going to school consistently so he eventually dropped out. "I didn't really have a plan or know what I wanted to do at the time," he said. "It didn't make sense to pay for school without having a clear direction of what I wanted to study."

During this time (late 1990s) there was a huge demand for computer (hardware and software) and information technology (IT) skills in the job industry. Specifically, a Windows-based knowledge was highly sought after by employers. Trade/technical/vocational schools started offering computer-based training programs to teach necessary skills related to a specific job. The job market was drastically changing at the turn of the century with companies desperately seeking individuals with computer/technical knowledge.

Dennis knew he needed some sort of education or training on his resume to help boost his employment opportunities. He discovered a technical training school called The Academy in Miami that offered a wide array of courses covering computer skills. He remembers paying around $7,000 for a package that provided him with classes on how to repair and build computers along with other hardware and software certificate programs. Dennis also earned Microsoft certifications in database and server administration.

As a result of his technical training Dennis landed a job with CompuPay, a payroll services company. Human resources (HR) and payroll software was a $10.8 billion industry in the U.S. in 2020. The role of installing software for CompuPay's clients was Dennis's introduction to the payroll industry. His ascent within the company eventually moved him and his family to the Tampa/St. Petersburg area. Over the next seven years Dennis worked his way up by training, troubleshooting, and processing data for third-party vendors who became clients of CompuPay's payroll software. Then, in 2004 he had the opportunity to open and run an office in Atlanta. After starting as a one-man band, Dennis became an office manager and built a sales staff of around eight employees.

In 2007 a colleague mentioned a potential opportunity with a competing payroll service provider—Ultimate Software. Looking for more financial stability, Dennis applied for an opening but never heard back. Later that year he landed a new job with Administaff, a human resources and administrative services company. Then nearly a year after he applied with Ultimate Software, they finally called back and hired him as a software consultant. With Ultimate Software offering a human capital management system, Dennis worked with clients in a consulting role providing payroll, HR, benefits, and recruitment needs for their companies.

In 2011 Dennis left Ultimate Software to work for Appirio, an information technology consulting company. About two months later Ultimate came calling for him to come back by enticing him with a consultant director position and a 35% salary increase from what he was previously earning. In his new role, Dennis worked with bigger clients (companies with 100,000+ employees) and was required to travel more extensively.

Dennis was promoted in 2018 to a senior software consultant working more exclusively with internal clients. In this role he serves as the first resource for company's consultants in the field. He no longer travels and works 100% remotely from the comfort of his home. During his 13 years at Ultimate Software, Dennis has had the opportunity to partner with many prominent clients such as Tesla, Google, MLB, NBA, Marriott, Yamaha, Sony, and Samsung.

"There are so many successful people who never went to college," Dennis said. "It's fine either way, but college isn't for everyone."

* * *

Final Thoughts

While a traditional four-year degree is not for everybody, trade school can offer a compelling career path and is a tremendous option that many people overlook when deciding what to do after high school. A four-year degree is expensive, and not suited to everyone's learning style and skill set. If you're a hands-on learner, excited by the prospects of getting out of the classroom and starting to work immediately after high school, trade school is a relatively inexpensive alternative education that may work well for you.

Young people aren't the only ones who can benefit from technical college. If you're ready for a career change or are interested in trying a new career after you retire, exploring technical college may be a great first step. You might find that you're perfectly suited for a career you've never considered before.

One thing that annoyed me about attending traditional college was being forced to take "core classes" that I had no interest in. At the time I was passionate about sports broadcasting, journalism, writing, and media studies and was perplexed as to why I had to take microbiology, art appreciation, algebra, and philosophy. All a colossal waste of time and money—especially since I knew exactly what I wanted to do. I understand some students have difficultly declaring a major, or even change their major multiple times, but if you know what you want to study, then why not explore the trade school option?

CONTINUING/PROFESSIONAL EDUCATION

Full discloser: I'm biased toward this option because I spent nearly five years working for my alma mater's College of

Professional Education and witnessed firsthand how this
education route changed people's lives.

Many colleges and universities offer continuing or professional education/training programs (also referred to as professional development) that provide non-degree courses designed to increase your work-based skills. Many of these professional education programs will award you a certificate upon completion and most offer an in-person or online learning platform. Whether you are seeking an industry certification, a digital badge in leadership, or skills training to enter a new field, each of these are obtainable through continuing and professional education courses at a fraction of the cost and time of traditional college. Popular professional certificate-based programs include offerings in healthcare, technology, business, legal, and hospitality/culinary. On average, many of these courses range from three to 18 months and cost $500 to $10,000.

For example, if you are enthusiastic about saving lives and caring for others you might want to enter the healthcare field. Instead of spending four to six years potentially paying more than $100,000 at a traditional college, you could enroll in a professional certificate program for one of the following: certified nursing assistant, EKG technician, medical assisting, pharmacy technician, and medical interpreter, etc. These programs range from about $2,000 to $8,000 with a time commitment of three to 18 months.

The technology industry is always a hot job market. These certificate-based programs might expedite your route to landing gainful employment: CompTIA, Cisco CCNA, bookkeeper, ethical hacker, information systems security, AutoCAD, web design and development, and social media marketing. Additionally, if you are interested in the legal field but not interested in the cost and time it takes to earn a law degree, then studying to become a paralegal might be a good fit. Again, you can do this through obtaining a paralegal professional certificate. Most programs take approximately two years to complete and cost around $5,000.

Benefits of Professional Education Courses

- **Cost** – Continuing and professional education courses offered by a college or university typically cost much less than a degreed program. On average, classes run anywhere between $500 to $10,000.

- **Time** – Earning a professional certificate will save you significant time versus the tradition college route of four to six years. Certificate programs generally take around three months to two years to complete. Some courses can be as short as six weeks.

- **Flexibility** – Continuing and professional education programs cater greatly to working adults and those with families. Courses offer flexibility with day and night classes along with in-person and online learning. Some training classes are even offered on the weekends.

- **Minimal requirements** – Most professional certificate/development programs have very little prerequisites involved with enrollment. There are no transcripts from previous school requirements nor will you have to provide GPAs, SAT, or ACT scores. However, most registration offices prefer students to be at least 18 years old to enroll.

Final Thoughts

If you know specifically what you are interested in pursuing —healthcare, legal, business, technology— earning a professional certificate from an accredited college or university could save you a tremendous amount of time and money in an effort to land employment in your preferred field. Explore the options that your local universities have available. You just might be pleasantly surprised.

APPRENTICESHIPS

Did you know? Many trades don't require any paid tuition to learn a marketable skill on the job, and some will even pay you to learn through an apprenticeship program. That's right! Welcome to the world of apprenticeships—the structured training programs which provide a chance to work towards a qualification while helping obtain the skills and knowledge needed to succeed in a specific industry.

Securing employment earlier means there's lots of potential to progress in a career quickly and also presents the opportunity to earn a good salary much earlier in life. Additionally, hands-on training provides a real chance to put skills into practice and helps a person gain more confidence in a professional working environment.

What is an Apprenticeship?

The U.S. Department of Labor (DOL) defines an apprenticeship as an employer-driven, "learn-while-you-earn" model that combines on-the-job training, provided by the employer that hires the apprentice, with job-related instruction in curricula tied to the attainment of national skills standards.

The model also involves progressive increases in an apprentice's skills and wages.

The DOL further stated: Apprenticeship programs keep pace with advancing technologies and innovations in training and human resource development through the complete involvement of employers in the educational process. While it is used in traditional industries such as construction and manufacturing, apprenticeships are also instrumental for training and development in growing industries, such as healthcare, information technology, transportation and logistics, and energy.

* * *

Real-Life Example: Culinary Program

My previous employer, KSU's College of Professional Education, offers a fantastic and highly respected Culinary Apprenticeship Certificate Program. The course runs about nine months and costs just under $10,000. It offers a unique blend of classroom-based teaching (in a restaurant-style kitchen) by professional chefs along with an apprenticeship. The apprenticeship aspect of the program places students on a rotation system that provides them with different types of work experience within the culinary industry including placement at various restaurants and catering companies. The students are paid for their work at the apprenticeship sites and the majority of them are offered jobs upon completion of the course.

The program has produced many success stories with graduates who have opened their own restaurants and catering companies, launched food truck businesses, and become renowned chefs. If you have completed high school and have identified you want to enter the restaurant/culinary/hospitality industry, then a program like this might be worth considering over a traditional college.

. . .

Apprenticeship Benefits

- **Earn While You Learn** - While gaining an invaluable knowledge base and skill set you will also not be accruing student loans or paying tuition fees, which equals no debt. You'll be paid a salary by your employer, and the government tends to cover the cost of the training for most young people.

- **Hands-on Career Training** - Apprentices receive practical, on-the-job training in a wide variety of occupations and industries, such as healthcare, cosmetology, construction, information technology, transportation, energy, restaurant/hospitality, and advanced manufacturing.

- **Education** - Apprentices receive hands-on training resulting in improved skills and competencies as well as the potential to earn college credit toward an associate or bachelor's degree.

- **Career** - Once the apprenticeship is complete, workers are on their way to a successful long-term career with a competitive salary and with little or no educational debt.

- **National Credential** - When an apprentice graduates from a career training program, he or she earns a certified portable credential accepted by industries and employers across the U.S.

* * *

Real-Life Story: Jenna Ellis

My sister, Jenna Ellis, is a great example of someone who has succeeded in discovering her professional passion through an apprenticeship program. After high school Jenna enrolled at a university near her home but after two years of the traditional university life, she decided it wasn't for her. She was interested in creative art classes but was finding the core requirement courses were becoming increasingly more difficult.

"I was paying for college while working full time and living at home," Jenna said. "It made me really think, 'Is this what I want to do?' I was either going to be an art teacher or a starving artist and neither of those options intrigued me."

While attending college Jenna worked full time at a jewelry kiosk in a nearby mall. Later she landed a position as a makeup artist with Rich's department store. Jenna then worked for another makeup brand called Prescriptives before getting on with Estée Lauder—eventually being promoted to counter manager. A few years later Jenna felt like there were no more opportunities for advancement into creative roles so she began searching for another endeavor.

Jenna accepted a receptionist job at a hair and makeup salon. After working there for a few months, the owner asked if she wanted to be his apprentice. She had never thought of becoming a hair stylist before this point. Jenna committed to the two-year apprenticeship program and shadowed her boss. She received valuable, hands-on experience and was paid an hourly rate plus tips. "I loved it," Jenna said. "After the apprenticeship I was offered a full-time position at the salon." In her full-time role she was paid on a commission basis.

To become an officially licensed hair and makeup stylist Jenna was required to take the Georgia State Board examination. Upon successful completion she earned her license as a master cosmetologist, which must be renewed every two years in Georgia.

After working at the salon for four years Jenna desired to branch out on her own as an independent contractor by renting a booth at another salon called Serendipity Designs. This allowed her to set her own hours and rates and build clientele. She worked at Serendipity for nearly five years as a professional hair and makeup artist.

Now Jenna works for Ulta Beauty, a nationwide beauty salon retail chain doing hair and makeup. She is paid on a sliding commission scale, which means the more money you make, the higher commission you receive. She wants to stay with Ulta because of the employee benefits which includes health insurance. Jenna explained that it's rare to find a salon that provides its employees with benefits. She has now been with Ulta for five years.

Jenna's story is a great example of developing a relevant, recession-proof skill that will always be in demand. In fact, when the COVID-19 pandemic hit, one of the things people had to figure out was how to get a haircut. Many, like myself, tried to cut their own hair...and...well....that was a mistake.

* * *

Final Thoughts

If you're curious about the skills you could learn and the apprenticeships that may be available in your area, Apprenticeship.gov offers an apprenticeship finder tool that helps you locate these opportunities in any ZIP code nationwide. Common fields that offer paid apprenticeships include plumbing, pipefitting, carpentry, and ironwork, but there are plenty of other fields that offer this type of opportunity.

The DOL reports that the average apprentice starts out making $15 per hour while they learn, which sounds a lot better than borrowing money to attend school for four years or longer, right?

JOIN THE MILITARY

There are many practical benefits to joining a branch of the military. In addition to a competitive salary, free healthcare, and minimal living expenses, the military will cover your tuition while in service. Additionally, soldiers have access to a variety of online learning options and there are satellite classrooms on many bases. Once your service is complete, you can also use the GI Bill to pay for part of your tuition. The military also offers retirement with benefits after 20 years of service.

Serving your country is not only a tremendous honor but there are numerous benefits including:

- A salary with increasing pay the longer you're in the service
- Diverse training that's transferable to your future career
- Potential to have your college paid for
- Free healthcare and nearly free living costs
- Free travel across the United States and overseas

I know a few people who joined the military out of high school and they all love the discipline and organization it gives them. You don't need a college degree to join the military. By joining the military you're giving back to your country and you'll have a stable job for the first few years out of high school. Plus, they offer on-the-job training for a number of potential career fields you can transition to after your service ends.

* * *

Real-Life Story: Brent Johnson

My friend Brent Johnson is the perfect example of someone who succeeded professionally by maximizing his military benefits to pay for schooling, which led to an apprenticeship. Brent has been an auto mechanic for 30 years and has been fixing my cars for at least 20 of those years. For the past 13 years he has also been a firefighter. Brent has always been a car guy and knew at an early age that he wanted to work with cars. He enrolled in Gwinnett Technical College in Lawrenceville, Georgia, to pursue an associate degree in automotive training.

As a U.S. Army veteran, Brent qualified for VA Education Benefits through the GI Bill. This would cover half of his college expenses. To cover the other half of his educational expenses, Brent discovered that Gwinnett Tech offered a dealership sponsorship program with Atlanta-based Honda car dealerships. The program, known as the Honda PACT (professional automotive career training), is designed to provide students the skills needed to become qualified to enter the Honda and Acura dealer network. By becoming enrolled in the PACT program through his school Brent received scholarship money for the remainder of his education expenses.

In the two-year PACT program Brent learned to maintain, diagnose, and repair two of the world's most popular brand of automobiles. Students have the opportunity to earn 10 Honda and Acura certifications all taught by Honda certified instructors, and the ability to earn at least two ASE certifications through the National Institute for Automotive Service Excellence. Brent was also taught the fundamentals of electrical, engines, steering, and suspension.

As part of the PACT program Brent was placed in a Honda dealership (Carey Paul Honda in Snellville, Georgia) in a work-based training environment. He went to school in the mornings and worked at the dealership in the afternoons and evenings. After he completed his associate degree Brent was hired on full time by Carey Paul Honda as an ASE certified mechanic. Several years later he earned his certification to become a master technician. Brent worked at the Honda dealership for 15 years before branching off and starting his own repair shop business that he runs out of his home.

To become a firefighter, applicants only need a high school diploma. However, before you are officially hired you must complete an EMT school certification along with firefighter school training. Brent works one, 24-hour shift every three days and has been elevated to a sergeant (driver engineer) position.

Brent's story shows that if you have identified career paths that you are truly passionate about you might be able to find an alternative, and much less expensive route, to achieve your professional goals.

* * *

Final Thoughts

Joining the military isn't a decision to be taken lightly. It can be a dangerous occupation. Additionally, you aren't in control of your time. Someone else dictates what you do and when you do it until your service is up. On the flip side your time in the service will undoubtedly be the most impactful of your life. You'll make lifelong friends and forever view the world differently. In many cases the military will take a shy, insecure kid and transform him or her into a mature, confident adult.

FREE ONLINE LEARNING/MOOCS

Want an Ivy League education without forking up $200,000 to pay for it? Free online courses may be beneficial for you. Online learning sites like Coursera, Harvard Extension, edX, and others have made it cost-free and simple to gain new knowledge. This way you're getting a feel for what subjects you're passionate about before wasting time paying for college and switching your major four times in your freshman year.

.   .   .

What are MOOCS?

MOOC stands for massive open online courses. Traditional MOOCs are free online university courses offered by colleges all over the world that are normally not eligible for credit. Their enrollment can run upwards of 100,000+ students and anyone can register. After registering, students will typically work at their own pace to watch informative lectures and lessons, complete assignments, and take exams.

The MOOC market is booming. Ivy League schools like Yale and Harvard are beginning to offer free and open access to select courses in order to make themselves more accessible. Completing one of these courses may show employers that you're motivated and willing to learn. If you're in the final round of interviews, this may set you apart from the others, but this alone won't land you a job.

The free online learning route could serve as a tremendous benefit to high school upperclassman or recent graduates as they explore what they might and might not be interested in before jumping into college. Another option is to potentially forgo college altogether by using the knowledge and skills learned from these classes. You can also use what you learned from a free online course to pursue another alternative to traditional college mentioned in this chapter.

MOOC Topics

You can find a plethora of subjects on free online learning platforms such as:

- Fundamental Marketing
- Content Marketing
- Social Media Marketing
- Email Marketing
- SEO

- Sales
- Ecommerce
- Coding & Developer Courses
- Personal & Professional Development Courses
- Design
- Business & Finance

Final Thoughts

Before doing research for this book, I had no idea that this option was available. The internet can be a great and powerful tool, so don't take it for granted! Free online courses can improve your current skill set and make you a better employee. It also shows initiative, which managers like. However, don't solely rely on these types of courses to land you that dream job. I realize that not everyone is wired for online learning but it's definitely worth looking into.

WORKING — ON-THE-JOB TRAINING

Contrary to popular opinion, you can skip college entirely and can begin working right away with a high school degree. As previously stated, college isn't for everyone and that's OK. Remember nearly 40% of high school graduates never attend a university and only 60% of people who start college obtain a degree. If you've completed high school and have already developed a passion that can be transferred into a specific line of work, then college might be a waste of time for you.

Start a Business

There are so many ways to jumpstart your life and your career. Nearly 30 million small business owners operate in the

U.S. alone. Thanks to the internet, the barriers to starting your own business have never been lower. A storefront—with expensive rent, utilities, inventory, and employees—is no longer necessary to sell goods or services. A computer and an internet connection are all you need to start a business from anywhere in the world.

While you're young, you have few assets and time on your side. That means you don't have a lot to lose, so now might be the perfect time window to launch that website, build that app, or start freelancing.

* * *

Real-Life Story: Michael White

My friend Michael White is a great example of someone who has succeeded professionally without obtaining a college degree. After graduating from Sprayberry High School in Marietta, Georgia, Michael desired to attend the Art Institute of Atlanta and study film and video production. However, with the school being in the private sector Michael and his family could not afford the nearly $25,000 a semester tuition rates at the time. Instead of going into debt, Michael went to work.

After bouncing around from several food service and retail industry jobs Michael realized those roles weren't for him. "I didn't like dealing with that type of customer," he said. A friend who was employed at Atlanta's Piedmont Hospital performing networking and IT-related work alerted Michael of a similar opportunity there. He joined the staff as a field technician where he learned networking with phones, as well as computers, along with voice and data cabling. Voice and data networking uses trends and technologies for merging voice and data communication on a single network. It is part of a broader multiservice networking concept that combines all types of communication onto a single network to connect two or more computers or to share printers, scanners, etc.

With only a year at the hospital job it proved to be an excellent training ground for Michael. He learned the rules of infrastructure cabling which he still uses today. It was on-the-job training in its finest form. At the end of the first year a networking cable opportunity came up with a company called OSP. Then after soaking up more on-the-job training skills and courses, Michael moved on to work with U.S. Data. He said he took that job for the opportunity to get training and learn more about fiber and cameras as a result of changing technologies. Coincidentally, he later began dating a young lady whose father had his own low voltage cabling business. Michael then started working for his future father-in-law at Georgia Wire Services and continued his education while polishing his skill set. Over the course of the next five years, Michael earned several continuing education certifications to further his career.

During his time at Georgia Wire Services Michael gained project management experience while working for a client named Cellular Specialties, Inc. (CSI). After working with CSI for three years, and with the CSI account contract ending, the company severed its ties with Georgia Wire Services. Michael was bummed, but then a phone call changed his life. It was his former partner Mike from CSI. He wanted to work exclusively with Michael and requested that he start his own company. Since he learned how to manage company finances from previous owners he worked under, or as he says, "I learned what not to do with my own business," Michael agreed and CSI became his first client. A month later Michael, just 27 at the time, cashed out his entire 401(k) and savings—totaling around $10,000. He used the money to buy a van, secure a business name, and launch a website. As a result, Cable Able Technologies was born in April of 2007.

Michael is the sole employee of his company, but he does

hire subcontractors as needed. Over the past 13 years Cable Able has grown significantly. NASA, Boeing, Dynetics, Coca-Cola, Pepsi, Mary Kay, Snap-On, Toyota, Kia, BMW, Siemens, Scientific Games, and Walmart are just some of the high-profile companies Michael has worked with.

Michael's story shows that by identifying your passions, while seizing opportunities and taking risks, you can enjoy a successful professional career without holding a college degree.

* * *

Intern/Volunteer

If there is a particular company you are interested in working for and they don't have any full-time positions open, call their human resources department and ask if you can intern or volunteer. This could create an opening for you to get your foot in the door in order to gain valuable networking opportunities with the company's top decision-makers. It's the old saying, "It's not *what* you know, but *who* you know." Many companies place great value in their interns and volunteers and will hire them before interviewing strangers off the street. Plus, you'll be gaining real-world experience and invaluable connections in the process.

Careers that Don't Require a Degree

Many occupations do not require a college education and earning a degree will do nothing at all to improve your chances of getting a job or advancing. The following occupations don't require a college degree and some of them pay extremely well:

- Commercial pilot
- Sound engineering technician
- Insurance sales rep

- Medical assistant or secretary
- Criminal detective
- Physical trainer
- Loan officer
- Massage therapist
- Graphic designer
- Web developer
- Computer coder
- Optician
- Casino gaming manager
- Power plant operator
- Transportation inspector
- Personal care aide
- Subway and streetcar operator
- Farmer or rancher

Final Thoughts

Obviously, you need the necessary skills for jobs like graphic designer and web developer, but the aforementioned list or Michael's story goes to show that not having a college degree doesn't get in your way for most jobs. While your peers are paying to learn in college, you're getting paid to learn on the job. Additionally, you could be earning a full-time salary with benefits four-to-six years before your friends who take the college route.

12

NOW WHAT?

Believe you can and you're halfway there. - Theodore Roosevelt

---

I f you've made it this far, congratulations, you are serious about obtaining some form of higher education while avoiding student loan debt in the process. Paying for college is one of the largest, single expenses that most individuals, or families, will make in a lifetime. Although college is usually a good bet, there is also risk involved. I hope by reading this book you've come to the realization that having to mortgage your financial future to either send your child to college, or attend college yourself, may not be a wise decision.

"We've been telling everyone college is the golden ticket," *Making College Pay* author Beth Akers told Yahoo Finance Live. "Not really. It's an investment, and like any other investment you need to make critical decisions and use economics to make sure that you're making a choice that's going to pay off for you."

The bottom line is to treat college like any other decision—weigh the benefits against the cost.

* * *

In this book you've learned about the student debt crisis and how you should want no part of it, the *real* cost of college, how to pay for college, how to save while in college, and alternatives to traditional college.

Additionally, it is my desire that by reading this book you have not bought the lie that student loans are a necessity. As you've discovered from the individual stories (including yours truly), *IT IS POSSIBLE* to go to school without going into debt.

Think about it. Would you rather work hard to avoid student loan debt or work hard for decades after you graduate to pay off student loan debt?

* * *

ACTION PLAN:

Start working as a teenager – Your teenage years are an ideal time to work and start saving money for your potential higher education opportunities. Also, these years are probably the easiest time to save money because you are living at home with very little expenses. Don't wait until after you've graduated high school to start researching and planning for the cost of college.

Get to know your high school guidance counselor – This is certainly a regret of mine. I don't remember ever meeting with my high school guidance counselor. What an extremely valuable resource that I wasted. Your guidance counselor is there to help you succeed in a variety of ways. A counselor is tasked with assisting students in making academic and career plans including college applications, jobs, and scholarships.

Begin to determine your direction – Remember college is best suited for individuals who have identified a specific career path. It is not a time to "discover yourself"—it's simply too expensive. When I enrolled in undergraduate school it was because I had no idea what else I was supposed to do at the time. And when I was a graduate student many of my classmates were there because they didn't know what they wanted to do. We have a term for these people—*career students*. While there is no shame in earning higher education degrees, the issue is racking up tens of thousands of more student loan debt in doing so. They are literally buying time to "discover themselves" and many graduates don't end up working in the field of their degree anyway. Your desire to go to college should begin with a career option(s) that actually requires a college degree.

Connect with your college academic advisors and scholarship counselors – This is yet another regret of mine (see high school guidance counselor). Colleges and universities have dedicated staff members whose sole job is to ensure your success. Once you begin school ask where the scholarship office is and make an appointment to meet with a counselor. Their job is to help you find scholarship money. Even if you've already enrolled in college you can still apply for scholarship money to help defray the cost of future studies. Don't take this for granted!

Once you declare a major you should also have an academic advisor assigned to you. The only time I remember meeting with an academic advisor was when I was a senior declaring to graduate. Don't be like me. Get to know all the vital resource members of your school and see how they can help you financially and academically.

Meet with a career coach – A career coach can help you determine and focus on your areas of passion and what job industries/markets they translate to. I can vouch for the value of having a career coach. At several different times in my life a coach has helped me develop clarity on my goals and ambitions of what I desired from a job and career.

Additionally, a career coach is an unbiased advocate who provides objective feedback tailored to your search and career goals. A professional mentor of this type will get to know your skills and aptitude as an employee then work with you to achieve your goals. One element a coach may implement is the use of personality tests like DISC, Myers-Briggs Type Inventory (MBTI), or Enneagram, and career assessment tests like the MAPP (Motivational Appraisal Personal Potential). Career assessments are perfect for students, graduates, and working adults. You'll get a wealth of information to help find the right career that matches your unique assessment profile. Among the factors a career test may cover include skills, strengths, interests, emotional intelligence, values, personality traits, and motivations.

* * *

You *CAN* do this!
　I *BELIEVE* in you!
　Jason.

AFTERWORD

By Timothy Norris, Co-Author of "The Debt Slayers," Co-founder of Cultivate Freedom & Legacy

When I embarked on college and graduate school over a decade ago, I had no idea that path would lead to one of the biggest money lessons of my life. As a millennial, eager to become the person I dreamed of becoming, I went to college to equip myself with the skill sets needed to reach my goal of becoming an architect. During this six-year period, I made amazing friends and built invaluable relationships that are still a part of my life to this day. The memories made throughout my matriculation has ultimately molded me into the person I am today. I am truly grateful for the education and experiences awarded to me from the fine institutions I attended.

However, it is important to note that I accumulated over a whopping $100,000 in student loans to "become the person I dreamed of becoming." Well, close to that person since I changed my major from engineering to business administration. In all seriousness, let the astronomical six-figure price tag of my college tuition sink in for a moment. I could have traveled to each continent on earth twice for less than this amount. Or even purchased three Tesla Model 3s for the same amount. This tuition cost was more than what an entry-level architect made for close to three years at that time. I had essentially amassed debt the size of a mortgage. OK, I think you get the point. My degrees soon became a memento that signified debt, the opposite of liberation.

Unfortunately, my experience was not too different from many other millennials who attended college during this period of rapid increase in tuition cost and burden, which would pile up to become the notorious $1.7 trillion student loan crises today. All I wanted from college was a rewarding professional career that would allow me to fulfill passion while achieving financial goals. Instead, I received an unstable entry into the workforce during the Great Recession and a ton of debt. It wasn't long after accumulating over $100K in debt that I married the most amazing woman ever, who was also plagued by massive student loan debt. Collectively, we had well over $300K in student loan debt alone.

Realizing the amount of debt I had collected was a pivotal moment in my life that changed me for the better. At least that was after I stopped blaming the "broken education system" which allowed young teenagers like myself the opportunity to take out student loans without truly knowing the full impact it would have on their future. For example, I experienced daily depression and anxiety attacks from knowing that my new family's debt was growing by a shameful $1,000 in interest per month. However, my wife and I chose to take complete ownership over our financial situation which seemed bleak at the time. We were equally committed to this task, so we got on a zero-based budget and put together a debt-snowball plan that we followed until we reached financial freedom. We had paid off a mind-blowing $429,768.17 in debt within 48 months!

I share this piece of my own personal story in hopes to not

only to inspire others that debt freedom is obtainable, but to also give people an opportunity to learn from my history so that they avoid student loan debt to the best of one's ability. You see, I did not accumulate massive debt because of a "broken education system." I accumulated this debt because I did not have a financial plan that was data driven and followed tightly. If I did, maybe I would only have had collected 50% of the debt or even 25%. Maybe none at all. I don't know and I never will know because I did not have a budget or specific financial plan for college. It took a crushing family debt of close to a half a million dollars for me to get on an actionable plan. Take ownership over your financial future now by getting on a detailed budget ASAP. Your future freedom and legacy depend on it!

AN INVITATION

My hope in writing this book is to inspire and encourage you to realize that *IT IS POSSIBLE* to walk across that stage and be handed a diploma instead of receiving bills in the mail for student loan debt to be repaid. Additionally, it was my desire to show you that life can be lived in a way that does not include feeling stress, anxiety, and depression over money. That's why I created a website to accompany this book. I invite you to continue this journey with me at yourmarginmatters.com. There you can subscribe to my blog and be alerted each time I publish. Additionally, I've launched a YouTube channel that will help carry on many of the stories you read about in this book. You can find me on YouTube by searching "Jason Brown Margin Matters" and subscribing to my channel.

You can do this!

Jason

GLOSSARY

- **Apprenticeship** – a program or position in which someone learns a trade by working under a certified expert.
- **Bankruptcy** – the state of being bankrupt (of a person or organization) declared in law unable to pay outstanding debts. The state of being completely lacking in a particular quality or value.
- **Curriculum** – the subjects comprising a course of study in a school, college, or university.
- **Default** – failure to meet financial obligations, as when a borrower misses or stops making monthly loan payments.
- **Deferment** – the action or fact of putting something off to a later time; postponement. A deferment period is an agreed-upon time during which a borrower does not have to pay the lender interest or principal on a loan. Depending on the loan, interest may accrue during a deferment period, which means the interest is added to the amount due at the end of the deferment period.

- **Forbearance** – a form of repayment relief granted by a lender that temporarily postpones payments due from a borrower, while interest on the loan typically continues to accrue.
- **Deferment vs. Forbearance: What's the Difference in regard to Student Loans?** – Both allow you to temporarily postpone or reduce your federal student loan payments. The main difference is if you are in deferment, no interest will accrue to your loan balance. If you are in forbearance, interest will accrue on your loan balance.
- **Human capital** – the collective skills, knowledge, and experience possessed by an individual or population, viewed in terms of their value or cost to an organization or country.
- **Indentured servitude** – is a form of labor in which a person agrees to work without salary for a specific number of years through a contract for eventual compensation or debt repayment.
- **Inflation** – a persistent, substantial rise in the general level of prices related to an increase in the volume of money and resulting in the loss of value of currency (opposed to deflation).
- **Juris doctorate degree** – This is the highest education available in the legal profession in the United States and is considered a professional degree.
- **Listserv** – an application that distributes messages to subscribers on an electronic mailing list.
- **Matriculate** – to enroll in a college or university as a candidate for a degree.
- **MOOCS** (massive online learning courses) – a course of study made available over the internet without charge to a very large number of people.

- **Spillover benefits** – are free benefits that third parties or society receive from the actions of others.
- **Stipend** – a periodic payment, especially a scholarship or fellowship allowance granted to a student.
- **Subsidized vs. Unsubsidized loan: What's the difference?** *Subsidized* interest is paid by the Education Department while you're enrolled at least half time in college. *Unsubsidized* interest begins accruing as soon as the loan is disbursed, including while students are enrolled in school.

.

RESOURCES

STUDENT LOAN DEBT CRISIS:

Student Loan Debt Crisis Breakdown (Student loan debt has reached astronomical levels in the U.S., with 43 million Americans carrying an estimated $1.5 trillion in federal loan student debt and $119 billion in private student loans. The class of 2018 left school with an average of $28,950 in student loans. The financial burden of student loan debt proves heavier to bear for some borrowers than others.) https://www.thebalance.com/student-loan-debt-crisis-breakdown-4171739

Student Loan Debt Statistics For 2020 (The latest student loan debt statistics for 2020 have reached epic proportions. Student loan debt is now the second highest consumer debt category – behind only mortgage debt – and higher than both credit cards and auto loans.) https://www.makelemonade.co/student-loan-debt-statistics/

Mitch Daniels op-ed: A fix for student loan debt (Anyone who is unaware that we face a massive problem involving college student debt, contact Earth at your first convenience. The damage to young people's individual futures is compounded, we now know, by harm to the broader economy and society. Home ownership, marriage, childbearing, and new-business formation rates are all down among today's younger cohorts, and causal relationships to student debt have been established.) https://www.chicagotribune.com/opinion/commentary/ct-student-loan-debt-mitch-daniels-purdue-20150821-story.html

How student debt became a $1.6 trillion crisis (Advancements in technology, especially automation, are making it harder to earn a living wage without some type of advanced degree. Today, college graduates earn 80% more than those with just a high school diploma, on average. College is more expensive — and important — than ever before. And that dichotomy puts students in a difficult situation: do they risk going into debt they can't pay back or miss out on the benefits of a college degree?) https://www.cnbc.com/2020/06/12/how-student-debt-became-a-1point6-trillion-crisis.html

The Case Against Student Loan Forgiveness (Senators Chuck Schumer (D-NY) and Elizabeth Warren (D-MA) are calling on President-elect Biden to use his executive authority to cancel $50,000 in federal student loan debt per borrower. At a cost of roughly $1 trillion, that might be the most expensive policy ever enacted by executive order. Biden himself favors a smaller loan cancelation of $10,000 per borrower, but this would still cost upwards of $370 billion.) https://www.forbes.com/sites/prestoncooper2/2020/11/17/the-case-against-student-loan-forgiveness/?sh=77fcfbc464c6

Student Loans in Real Time (Total U.S. student debt hit $1.67 trillion at the start of 2020 and is tracking to reach $1.75 trillion by the end of the year. As the student debt amounts rise, so do the pressures on borrowers. Student loan options such as deferment, income-driven repayment plans or student loan refinancing can help borrowers manage their debt. But the numbers show America's student debt isn't going away anytime soon.) https://studentloanhero.com/student-loan-debt-clock/

The government can help people pay off student loans and be fair about it. Here's how. (What should be done about America's $1.6 trillion in outstanding student debt? There is more student debt than credit card debt or any other kind of debt except mortgage debt. Almost 45 million Americans have student debt, and the level is increasing. Seven in 10 seniors in the class of 2019 took out student loans.) https://news.yahoo.com/government-help-people-pay-off-100008692.html?.tsrc=daily_mail&uh_test=2_15

Student loan forgiveness may come with a tax bomb. How lawmakers might fix it (Student loan forgiveness is looking more like a possibility under President-elect Joe Biden, but an unintended consequence may emerge unless Washington intervenes: a tax on loan forgiveness. Biden has proposed creating a new program that would offer borrowers $10,000 of student debt relief for every year of national or community service, up to five years. The catch is that under ordinary circumstances, debt forgiveness or discharge—whether you're negotiating a balance on a credit card bill or offloading your home and underwater mortgage in a "short sale"—you'll be owing taxes on the amount forgiven.) https://www.cnbc.com/amp/2020/11/24/student-loan-forgiveness-may-come-with-tax-bomb-heres-what-you-should-know.html

Topic No. 431 Canceled Debt – Is It Taxable or Not? (If you borrow money and are legally obligated to repay a fixed or determinable amount at a future date, you have a debt. You may be personally liable for a debt or may own a property that's subject to a debt. If your debt is forgiven or discharged for less than the full amount you owe, the debt is considered canceled in the amount that you don't have to pay. The law provides several exceptions, however, in which the amount you don't have to pay isn't canceled debt. In general, if you have cancelation of debt income because your debt is canceled, forgiven, or discharged for less than the amount you must pay, the amount of the canceled debt is taxable and you must report the canceled debt on your tax return for the year the cancellation occurs.) https://www.irs.gov/taxtopics/tc431

Hoping for Student Loan Forgiveness Won't Pay the Bills (Federal student loan borrowers are waiting with bated breath to see whether loan forgiveness — which President-elect Joe Biden says he'll make a priority — becomes a reality. Industry experts say borrowers shouldn't count on it.) https://finance.yahoo.com/news/hoping-student-loan-forgiveness-won-212238849.html?.tsrc=daily_mail&uh_test=2_15

A Look at the Shocking Student Loan Debt Statistics for 2020 (It's 2021, and Americans are more burdened by student loan debt than ever. Among the Class of 2019, 69% of college students took out student loans, and they graduated with an average debt of $29,900, including both private and federal debt. Meanwhile, 14% of their parents took out an average of $37,200 in federal parent PLUS loans.) https://studentloanhero.com/student-loan-debt-statistics/

COLLEGE EXPENSES:

GoodCall Special Report: The Real Cost of College (There's almost nothing talked about more in higher education than the cost of college. The cost of a college degree increased 1,120% between 1978 and 2012—four times faster than the increase of the consumer price index. And as college tuition rises, so does student debt.) https://www.goodcall.com/education/college-costs/

13 sneaky costs of college — and how to keep them under control (When families think of financing a college education, they usually think about covering tuition costs. It's easy to home in on tuition — after all, it's an obvious, in-your-face expense. But tuition and fees don't make up the largest portion of the average cost of college attendance. In the College Board's most recent Trends in College Pricing, researchers found non-tuition-related expenses at public four-year schools account for 61% of a total $24,610 average cost of attendance.) https://www.businessinsider.com/hidden-costs-of-college-and-how-to-keep-them-under-control-2017-5

The Expense of Living On Campus vs. Off Campus (You're getting ready to embark on an exciting new journey: moving away for college. This often comes with a big decision, and you should keep the financial pieces in mind – how do the expenses of living on campus compare to off-campus living? There's no easy, straightforward answer to this until you explore and compare all of the available options in the town you're moving to.) https://www.collegeavestudentloans.com/blog/the-expense-of-living-on-campus-vs-off-campus/

The 50 Best Ways To Save Money In College And Live On A Tight Budget (The idea of saving money in college might sound impossible - but it's totally doable! For most college students, this is the first time really having to budget and manage money on your own. You might not know all the tips and tricks to make your money last. Before we can even have a conversation about saving money, it's essential that you understand the basics of budgeting and money organization. This is something that can be new to a lot of college students, but it's essential for financial success.) https://thecollegeinvestor.com/22453/save-money-in-college/#tab-con-56

How to Save Money in College (The more money you save during college, the more prepared you'll feel and the less you'll freak out about getting into the real world once you finally get your diploma. Plus, you won't have any of those lame student loan payments to worry about. And guess what? You don't even have to eat ramen every single night in order to save money and ditch the debt. There are plenty of ways to stack that cash. Let's talk about how you can cut costs on some of your biggest college expenses!) https://www.daveramsey.com/blog/how-to-save-money-in-college

This is how much a private college will cost when your baby grows up (New parents, take note: You will have to save six figures to send your child to a private college if tuition keeps increasing. It will cost today's newborns a whopping $302,700 to attend a four-year private college in 2036, according to a new calculation from the wealth-management company Wealthfront. That's up from $166,800 today.) https://www.marketwatch.com/story/this-is-how-much-a-private-college-will-cost-when-your-baby-grows-up-2018-08-29

To all parents: Don't break the bank to send your kids to their dream school (We are nearing the time of year when students announce their plans for college in the fall, and parents overextend themselves financially to make it happen, or feel very guilty for not doing so. Paying for college is one of the largest single expenditures that most individuals, or families, will make in a lifetime. Today, a typical bachelor's degree costs $85,000.) https://news.yahoo.com/parents-don-t-break-bank-080008531.html

SCHOLARSHIPS & GRANTS:

Remarkable Futures Scholarships (Scholarships at Chick-fil-A began when founder S. Truett Cathy set an empty mayonnaise jar on his restaurant counter to start a college fund for Team Member Eddie White. Since 1973, Chick-fil-A has invested more than $110 million in scholarships to help over 66,000 Team Members pursue a college education and achieve their remarkable future — whether it's with Chick-fil-A or elsewhere.) https://www.chick-fil-a.com/remarkable-futures-scholarships

No scholarship? Here's how to pay for college (Your child got into the college of their dreams. But the acceptance letter didn't mention any kind of scholarship. Now what? The good news is that most students receive some financial help paying for college, bringing the cost down from the school's "sticker price." Even without a scholarship, there are plenty of other forms of aid that can help you tackle the cost.) https://money.cnn.com/2017/04/25/pf/college/pay-for-college/index.html

$2.9 billion unused federal grant awards in last academic year (With average student debt levels rising to astronomical highs, making college affordable has become an increasingly complex challenge. Yet according to a study from *NerdScholar*, around $2.9 billion of federal grant money was left unclaimed after high school seniors eligible for Pell Grants -- which don't have be paid back -- neglected to complete the Free Application for Federal Student Aid (FAFSA) in the last academic year.) https://www.usatoday.com/story/college/2015/01/20/29-billion-unused-federal-grant-awards-in-last-academic-year/37399897/

16 Insider Facts about College Scholarships and Financial Aid (There are over 1 million scholarships available to students just like you every year — with a significant percentage of them going unclaimed! The same goes for federal and state financial aid – where more than $130 billion dollar is dispersed every year – even with millions of eligible students never taking the time to apply. Why?) https://myscholly.com/16-insider-facts-about-college-scholarships-and-financial-aid/

ALTERNATIVES TO TRADITIONAL COLLEGE:

Should I Go to a Technical or Trade School Instead of a College? – Pros & Cons (Deciding where you're going to go to school, or if you should go at all, can be overwhelming. The choice is even harder when you stop and think about the long-term implications. Should you go to a four-year university, a community college, get a degree online, or take a year off to work and think about what you want to do? These are all viable options. But another option that doesn't get quite as many headlines is going to a technical college.) https://www.moneycrashers.com/technical-trade-school-college/

Top 5 benefits of community college (Once you've decided to continue your education, the next step is choosing where you want to go to school. From less debt to smaller class sizes, community colleges have more to offer than you may realize. While the cost of college continues to rise across the board each year, community colleges offer a more affordable and accessible path to education. Whether you're having to borrow money for tuition, raise a family or work a full-time job, attending a community college may be the perfect way for you to continue your education.) https://clark.com/education/benefits-of-community-college/

APPLY FOR SCHOLARSHIP MONEY (Help Defray the Cost of College)

- Fastweb.com
- Scholarshippoints.com
- Unigo.com
- Scholarships.com
- Bigfuture.collegeboard.org
- Nextstudent.com
- Studentscholarships.org
- Scholarshipexperts.com
- Supercollege.com
- Collegeboard.org
- Niche.com
- Moolahspot.com

BOOK RECOMMENDATIONS:

- *Making College Pay: An Economist Explains How to Make a Smart Bet on Higher Education* by Beth Akers
- *The Price You Pay for College: An Entirely New Road Map for the Biggest Financial Decision Your Family Will Ever Make* by Ron Lieber
- *MillionDollarScholar: Winning the Scholarship Race* by Derrius Quarles
- *Debt-Free Degree: The Step-by-Step Guide to Getting Your Kid Through College Without Student Loans* by Anthony ONeal
- *The Ultimate Scholarship Book 2021: Billions of Dollars in Scholarships, Grants and Prizes* 13th Edition by Gen Tanabe
- *Paying the Price: College Costs, Financial Aid, and the Betrayal of the American Dream* by Sara Goldrick-Rab

- *The Graduate's Guide to Money: Tools for starting your financial journey on the right foot* by Tana Gildea
- *The Debt Slayers* by Timothy and Dr. LeAnn Norris
- *The AmerIcan Dream | HisStory In The Making* by David Lee Windecher

ACKNOWLEDGMENTS

I would like to thank several people who have greatly influenced the writing of this book.

The Interviewees: Derek Brott, Thomas Butterworth, Jenna Ellis, Katherine Hunt, Brent Johnson, Dennis Melendez, Amanda Parham, Dr. Steve Petty, Michael White, and David Lee Windecher. Your willingness to talk openly and honestly about a "taboo" subject when others wouldn't has added tremendous value to this book. Many people will learn many things from your financial and educational journeys.

The Influencers: God. His book, the Bible, provides a great source of information on money. Andy Stanley, founder of North Point Ministries, senior pastor of North Point Community Church. Your Balanced message series along with several other sermons on money have resonated with me. Dave Ramsey, author, radio host, and speaker. Your book *The Total Money Makeover* and radio show have been invaluable. Clark Howard, the king of cheap, the popular consumer expert and host of the nationally syndicated radio program the Clark

Howard Show. I have been a regular listener to your show and appreciate your creative frugalness.

The Coworkers: To my former coworkers at Kennesaw State University and my current coworkers at HNTB: Thank you for the support, interest, encouragement, and great questions about my book and the subject matter. I truly appreciate all the conversations we've had and hope that this book inspires you the way you have inspired me to finish it.

The Supporters: To all the people I've had a conversation with about writing this book. Thank you for the great questions, feedback, interest, support, and encouragement during the process. It was all that positive energy that pushed me through.

The Kennesaw State University Master of Arts in Professional Writing (MAPW) program: To all my MAPW instructors, classmates, and support staff: You have inspired, encouraged, and supported me beyond your wildest dreams. Thank you for your passion and unlimited creativity you allowed me to experience with you. By the way, hope you liked the cover shot of me graduating from our program!

Special Thanks: To Angela Walker who designed the cover of this book and to Charlotte Doolin who copyedited the words and provided helpful feedback on the content.

The Families: The Browns, Whites, Wikersons, Melendezes, Liggetts, Ellises, Reeveses, Behnkes—thank you for all your love, encouragement, and support over the years. My grandparents, William (Jack) and Florence Brown, and Floyd and Rudy Wilkerson—no one could ever have better grandparents than all of you. My parents, Melvin and Belinda Brown. Thank you for demonstrating wise financial choices by not being frivolous with what you had. A very special thanks goes out to Angie Hunt. Writing a book can be daunting but having a family member who is a New York Times best-selling author (and an author of over 200 books) certainly helps. Thanks for the guidance Angie. And to Amethyst Brown, my wife and ultimate teammate in life. Every editor needs an editor and you are the best I could ever ask for. Maddux and Kameron Brown, my sons. This book is for you. Now go learn something from it and do great things.

Celebrating earning my master's with my parents.

ABOUT THE AUTHOR

Jason Brown is the author of *Margin Matters: How to Live on a Simple Budget & Crush Debt Forever.* The book chronicles his journey of eliminating $75,000 of debt in three years and how to create more margin in your life no matter how much money you make.

During the day Jason works as a full-time copywriter/copy-editor for HNTB, a transportation consulting firm. He previously served as the copywriter for Kennesaw State University's College of Professional Education.

Prior to his roles at HNTB and KSU, Brown served in various capacities in sports media, marketing, and public relations where he worked for organizations such as ESPN, Fox Sports, Atlanta Braves, Atlanta Hawks, and the former-Atlanta Thrashers. Recently, he earned a Master of Arts in Professional Writing from KSU after earning a Bachelor of Science in Communication – Journalism/Media Studies from the same school.

Originally from Miami, Florida, Brown now makes his home in Roswell, Georgia, where he lives with his wife, Amethyst, their 5-year-old son, Maddux, and 1-year-old son, Kameron. He also collaborated with Hall of Fame Softball Coach Scott Whitlock on his memoir *I Wasn't Expecting All This.*

IN MEMORY OF
ROBERT SCOTT MYERS

You were loved by many and will be greatly missed.

Made in the USA
Columbia, SC
14 October 2021

47202022R00109